How to Run
Your Business
like a
girl

How to Run Your Business like a *girl*

Successful Strategies from Entrepreneurial Women Who Made It Happen

ELIZABETH COGSWELL BASKIN

Adams Media
Avon, Massachusetts

Published by
Adams Media, an F+W Publications Company
57 Littlefield Street, Avon, MA 02322. U.S.A.
www.adamsmedia.com

ISBN: 1-59337-455-0

Printed in Canada.

J I H G F E D C B A

Library of Congress Cataloging-in-Publication Data
Baskin, Elizabeth Cogswell.
How to run your business like a girl / Elizabeth Cogswell Baskin.
p.   cm.
ISBN 1-59337-455-0
1. Self-employed women—Handbooks, manuals, etc.
2. Businesswomen—Handbooks, manuals, etc. 3. Women-owned business
enterprises—Handbooks, manuals, etc. 4. Entrepreneurship.
5. Autonomy (Psychology) 6. Quality of work life. I. Title.
HD6072.5.B37 2005
658.02'2'082—dc22
2005007451

This publication is designed to provide accurate and authoritative information
with regard to the subject matter covered. It is sold with the understanding that
the publisher is not engaged in rendering legal, accounting, or other professional
advice. If legal advice or other expert assistance is required, the services of a
competent professional person should be sought.

　　　—From a *Declaration of Principles* jointly adopted by a Committee of the
American Bar Association and a Committee of Publishers and Associations

Many of the designations used by manufacturers and sellers to distinguish their
products are claimed as trademarks. Where those designations appear in this
book and Adams Media was aware of a trademark claim, the designations have
been printed in initial capital letters.

This book is available at quantity discounts for bulk purchases.
For information, please call 1-800-872-5627.

To Dr. Betty E. Cogswell,
my mother and an extraordinary woman.

Contents

———

xi . . . . . . Acknowledgments

xiii . . . . . Introduction

1 . . . . . .Chapter One: Do You Have the Entrepreneurial Itch?

2 . . . . The Entrepreneurial Risk: The Importance of Butterflies in Your Stomach

3 . . . . . . The Entrepreneurial Reason: Will It Make Your Life Better?

6 . . . . . . Patrice Tanaka of PT&Co.

6 . . . . . . Tara Mediate of KooKoo Bear Kids

7 . . . . . . Chellie Campbell of Financial Stress Reduction

7 . . . . . . Advice from Girlfriends Far and Wide

9 . . . . . .Chapter Two: The Principles That Guide the Business

11 . . . . . PT&Co.: Great Work, Great Workplace, Great Communities That Work

14 . . . . . KooKoo Bear Kids: Treat Your Customers like Your Friends

15 . . . . . Financial Stress Reduction: For the Love of Money, Fun, and Doing Good

17 . . . . . Instant Wisdom: On Guiding Principles

19 . . . . . Answers from Women Who've Done It

29 . . . . .Chapter Three: The Labor Pains of a Successful Startup

30 . . . . . PT&Co.: Buying Your Freedom

33 . . . . . KooKoo Bear Kids: Buying Lots of Stuff and Piling It in the Basement

36 . . . . . Financial Stress Reduction: Buying into Her Dream

38 . . . . . Instant Wisdom: On Startups

39 . . . . . *Answers from Women Who've Done It*

51 . . . . .Chapter Four: Grab Your Partner and Do-Si-Do

52 . . . . . PT&Co.: I'll Take a Baker's Dozen

55 . . . . . KooKoo Bear Kids: It's All in the Family

58 . . . . . Financial Stress Reduction: Thanks, but No Thanks

59 . . . . . Instant Wisdom: On Partnerships

60 . . . . . *Answers from Women Who've Done It*

65 . . . . .Chapter Five: Where You Go When You Go to Work

67 . . . . . PT&Co.: An Office with All the Extras

69 . . . . . KooKoo Bear Kids: The Business That Swallowed a Suburban Home

71 . . . . . Financial Stress Reduction: Moving Home to the Den

73 . . . . . Instant Wisdom: On Where to Put Your Office

74 . . . . . *Answers from Women Who've Done It*

85 . . . . .Chapter Six: How Was Your Day?

86 . . . . . PT&Co.: Dancing the Day Away

88 . . . . . KooKoo Bear Kids: The Best of Both Worlds—and Then Some

92 . . . . . Financial Stress Reduction: Daily Goal: Love Life

94 . . . . . Instant Wisdom: On the Quality of Your Life

96 . . . . . *Answers from Women Who've Done It*

Contents

107 . . .Chapter Seven: How to Be the Boss Without Being a Bitch

108.... PT&Co.: They Should Give an Award for This
115.... KooKoo Bear Kids: The Opposite of Micromanagement
118.... Financial Stress Reduction: No Employees? No Problem!
120.... Instant Wisdom: On Managing People
122.... *Answers from Women Who've Done It*

135 . . .Chapter Eight: What Doesn't Kill You Makes You Stronger

137.... PT&Co.: Being Solvent Versus Being Liked
141.... KooKoo Bear Kids: If We'd Known Then What We Know Now
142.... Financial Stress Reduction: When All Else Failed
145.... Instant Wisdom: On Surviving Difficult Times
147.... *Answers from Women Who've Done It*

159 . . .Chapter Nine: Cracking the Code on Marketing and Sales

162.... PT&Co.: Slow and Steady Wins the Race
166.... KooKoo Bear Kids: Buying Your Way into People's Homes
169.... Financial Stress Reduction: The Money Is in the Phone
174.... Instant Wisdom: On Bringing In Business
176.... *Answers from Women Who've Done It*

181 . . .Chapter Ten: Time to Start Your Own Startup

182.... The Startup: Where Do You Start?
184.... Business Plan, Schmizness Plan
184.... Name That Company
187.... www.YourCompanyHere.com
187.... To Inc. or Not to Inc.

188.... Let Me Give You My Card

191.... Your World Headquarters

192.... Hey Look, They Already Invented the Wheel

193.... How Many Highly Paid Execs Does It Take
to Change the Toner?

194.... The Beauty of Plan B(s)

196.... *Answers from Women Who've Done It*

205 . . . Epilogue

207 . . . Index

Acknowledgments

———

I owe plenty to the following people:

- Paula Walker, one of the women I admire most, and without whom I couldn't run my own business.
- The many women interviewed for this book, who so generously offered their stories and wisdom—and particularly Patrice, Tara, and Chellie.
- The friends and strangers who helped me find all these women.
- Everyone at Adams Media, but especially Danielle Chiotti and Gary Krebs.
- Jennifer Bull, my partner in Tribe, for running the show while I was writing this book.
- B.A. Albert, for making that first leap with me, and for also being so gracious about me bailing out later to go home and be a mom.
- Troy King, for his initial cover designs and the way he always makes my work look more brilliant than it really is.
- Leslie Burns, who transcribed hours of rambling conversations that normal people would never be able to follow.
- The women of The Pink Tea: old and new friends who inspire me with their power to make things happen in the world.

- ◆ The wise and loving women of Supper Club, who are behind me no matter what.
- ◆ Sam, for patiently stapling and drawing his own books beside me while I worked long hours on mine.
- ◆ And Steve. The man beside me, always.

Introduction

———

What does it mean to run your business like a girl? In the early part of my career, most of the women I knew, myself included, were trying to act as much as possible like the guys. We hoped no one would notice we were women (and we sure didn't let anybody call us girls). But it's also true that I have run my businesses differently from the men around me. I flat out didn't do a lot of things most businessmen probably consider essential. I'm not saying the way men do it is wrong. Some of the best role models I've had in business, and in life, have been men, and the same is probably true for you. But there are things women can teach about business that you aren't likely to hear from me.

Over time I've met more and more women entrepreneurs. And although we each have our own approaches to business, we are largely alike in the sense that we are *not* doing it by the book—at least not by the books they hand out at Harvard Business School.

The thing about running a business like a girl is that you never read anything about it. With most of the women I've met who run companies, there's some overlap in experience, but we all perceive ourselves as a little bit odd. Because we don't do business the way they teach it in Business 101, we think our company is just an anomaly that's somehow, against all odds, squeaking through to success.

So what do we do that's different? In the most broad and sweeping terms, women business owners tend to place more emphasis on relationships, intuition, and quality of life. In many cases, quality of life is the primary reason women start their companies, because they see being their own boss as the way to have more control over their own lives. The focus on and implementation of these three key emphases vary wildly from woman to woman and business to business. Women may do things differently from men, but they also do them differently from each other.

Women entrepreneurs make up their own rules as they go along. They don't feel compelled to do things the way other companies do them, or the way traditional business practices suggest they be done. Maybe women have less of their ego invested in running what others would consider a conventional company. Perhaps women take their personal values more seriously than the typical business practices that most guys would call good business. Or it could be that we just don't really care how somebody else thinks we ought to be doing things.

That willingness to ignore the generally accepted rules actually seems to be the main thread women entrepreneurs have in common. Women run their companies as they damn well please. When you get right down to it, maybe that's what it means to run your business like a girl.

How would you (or do you) run your own company? Probably not the exact same way the women in this book do it, because every female entrepreneur tends to follow her own rules. This book is meant to validate our approach, and to remind women that there's plenty of room for doing it your own way. Success is a destination reached by an endless number of paths. Your path is probably worthy of a book too. ■

Are you in earnest? Seize this very minute;
What you can do, or dream you can do, begin it;
Boldness has genius, power and magic in it.

Johann Wolfgang von Goethe

ᏬᏉ

1

Do You Have the Entrepreneurial Itch?

―――

If you want to start a company, then there's not much that will satisfy that desire except for starting a company. Some people are just not cut out to work for somebody else—at least, not for long. Others are so driven by a dream or an idea that they won't stop until it has come to fruition.

Following are some classic symptoms of the urge to become an entre-preneur. If you recognize more than one or two, you've got a serious case.

- ◆ You begin to notice that your talent and efforts have consistently made plenty of money for somebody else.
- ◆ You start to suspect that the people you've been working for might not be any smarter than you are.

- You doubt the ethical underpinnings of those who claim to be your leaders.
- You begin to crave more control over your life.
- You are increasingly frustrated by someone else controlling your time, and would much prefer to be the one deciding what you will do and when.
- You start to feel this craving for building real wealth rather than just collecting a salary.
- You find yourself rehearsing ways to explain to your mother that in fact the real risk is not starting something on your own but continuing to work for a company over which you have no control.
- You begin to believe that you could add to the world in a significant way through executing your idea for a new product, service, or way to do business.
- Starting your own company sounds like fun. (This is actually the best, and possibly the only real reason, to bite off more than you can easily chew.)

The Entrepreneurial Risk:
The Importance of Butterflies in Your Stomach

Yes, Virginia. Starting your own company is in many ways harder than punching the clock for someone else. Less boring, certainly, but you might not be able to leave at 5:00 for your spin class every day. (Then again, you might decide to make the 4:00 class once in a while.)

Starting your own company is an opportunity to write your own script. You get to decide everything. That's the good news. And on many, many occasions, you'll no doubt find that it's the bad news as well.

You will spend more time and energy on your own company than you can begin to believe. Not unlike having a child, if people had any realistic idea of what it would take, no one would ever do it. On the other hand, there are precious few entrepreneurs who say that what they really want in life is to go back to work for somebody else. Once you learn that secret handshake and pass through the portal to owning your own company, there is very rarely any desire to go back again.

If you're going to let a business enterprise consume so much of your life, you might want to make sure it's something that makes your heart pound. It's an excellent sign if, when you think about your business idea, you feel a sense of urgency to get it out there in the world before anyone else thinks of it. It's also a good sign if you can't stop daydreaming about it, and visualizing it, and scribbling notes about it. But if your business idea doesn't give you butterflies in your stomach, don't bother. If you're not completely in love with your idea for a company, it won't be worth the energy it will take to get it off the ground.

The Entrepreneurial Reason:
Will It Make Your Life Better?

When you talk to men and women who own their own businesses, one noticeable difference between the sexes lies in motivation. It's not that one sex works harder than the other, because all (successful) entrepreneurs work hard. But men and women are likely to have fundamentally different reasons for going into business in the first place.

Often, the men who start their own businesses are driven by a healthy ego and the desire to make money. Not that women don't have both of those, but typically these aren't the primary reasons women become entrepreneurs. Many women are prompted to start their own companies largely as a means to have more control over their lives. In many cases, they want to be available to their children at the unpredictable times that children tend to need parents. For other women, starting a company simply means the chance to create more balance in their lives.

There are plenty of reasons to start your own company, and both ego and money are perfectly good ones. But in the interest of life balance and personal happiness, ask yourself some probing questions before you haul yourself out of the corporate world to do your own thing: Will starting your own business make your life better? The entrepreneurial leap is worthy of some serious soul-searching. Owning a business will inevitably make your life more difficult in some ways, but so much better in others that you'll probably consider it a more-than-fair trade. Ask yourself the following:

- Will starting your own business make you feel more engaged, more useful, more powerful?
- Will it make your days more interesting?
- Do you have a hunch that you could make more money with your own company than you can at a salaried job?
- Are you okay with the possibility of making less money, at least for a while?
- Do you think that having your own company would be better or worse for your family, your relationships, and your life balance?
- Can you handle the emotional roller coaster of small business revenues?
- Are you generally an optimist? Can you get over setbacks quickly and keep moving?
- Are you okay with working extremely hard, and learning many new job functions as you go?
- Do you consider yourself high-energy and self-confident?
- Do you have the drive to be the one who makes things happen?
- Are you good at operating independently, without someone else to tell you what needs to be done?

- Could your company offer a product or service that's a positive contribution to our world? Or will you be able to help clients do the right thing?
- Do you have a burning desire to provide a fair and respectful place to work?

Finally, the true test as to whether or not you should start a company is this: Do you want to? If starting a company is what lights you up, if that's where your energy seems to be, if that's what is making you feel excited about getting out of bed in the morning, then do it.

You won't be the only one out there doing it on your own. One out of eighteen women in the United States is a business owner. Most of them are married; many have children. They're not all MBAs, nor are they teaming up with huge capital investors. Not all of them are even particularly knowledgeable about every aspect of building and operating a company. For the most part, women entrepreneurs are just regular people, like you and me. Don't think you have to wait until you have all the answers, or you may never do it. You really do not have to know everything. Believe me, a whole lot of us just make it up as we go along. Or we ask for help. One thing that women will do (and that men notoriously resist) is stop and ask for directions. We give and take advice easily about everything—from which schools are right for our kids to which eye cream is best for wrinkles.

One of the best ways to figure out how to do anything is to talk with someone who's already doing it. In the pages that follow, you'll learn how each of three women runs her own company like a girl. Each of them approaches her business in a unique way, and all of them do it differently from the way most typical men run their businesses. The three companies featured in the main body of this book represent a range of business models, and they're based in three different parts of the country.

You're going to get the kind of insider information you'd learn if you took each of the featured successful entrepreneurs out for a long lunch—with wine, and dessert, and plenty of time to talk over coffee afterward. These women will tell you the kinds of things they'd tell a friend about the real nitty-gritty of running a company. You're going to get a behind-the-scenes look at how and why they started their companies, what it took for them to succeed, how they handled the hard times, and what they love most about working for themselves. We'll cover a range of basic business topics, but also share off-the-cuff observations about the good, the bad, and the in-between.

Patrice Tanaka of PT&Co.

The first woman you'll meet is Patrice Tanaka, who runs PT&Co. (*www. ptanaka.com*), a Manhattan public relations agency with fabulous and expansive office space, filled with well-dressed employees racing around in fashionable suits and high heels. Patrice grew up in Hawaii, is well known and highly respected in the world of New York public relations, and seems to approach her business with joyful good humor and a Zen-like mindfulness.

Tara Mediate of KooKoo Bear Kids

The second woman is Tara Mediate, owner of KooKoo Bear Kids (*www. kookoobearkids.com*), a high-end children's catalog and Web site in suburban Atlanta. Her employees sometimes bring their children to work and her own kids occasionally Rollerblade through the warehouse. Tara makes no excuses for being a mom, regardless of how it might happen to interfere with business. She talks a million miles a minute, has more energy than seems reasonable for someone who clearly doesn't get much sleep, and admits she's still just getting the hang of e-mail.

Chellie Campbell of Financial Stress Reduction

Finally, there's Chellie Campbell, who operates her Financial Stress Reduction (*www.chellie.com*) workshops out of her home in Los Angeles and revels in having no employees at all.

Before getting into business, Chellie was a musical and comedic actress for fifteen years, so giving talks doesn't scare her one bit. "Every time I speak, I consider it like doing a one-woman show on money."

Chellie is a reformed workaholic whose former business was a bookkeeping company with over a dozen employees. Now she works a leisurely schedule that leaves time for her poker games and afternoon naps, all the while making plenty of money to live a prosperous life.

Advice from Girlfriends Far and Wide

Throughout this book you'll also find wisdom from numerous other women entrepreneurs who've been kind enough to offer their two cents. These women are from all over the country and they have started companies in a wide range of industries. They offer candid answers to questions about what they didn't know before they launched their companies, how much startup capital it took, the mistakes they won't make twice, and more.

As you read this book, you'll no doubt pick up a few pointers from each of these women. You may follow their wisdom in some cases; in others, you'll blaze your own trail. That's what it means to run your business like a girl. ■

We are not here merely to make a living.
We are here to enrich the world,
and we impoverish ourselves if we forget this errand.

Woodrow Wilson

∽

2

The Principles That Guide the Business

———

One of the best things about running your own company is that you get to do it your way. After all those years of watching people in management make decisions you thought were unethical, shortsighted, or just down-right dumb, you at last are the one calling the shots.

The downside of that is what my friend B.A. Albert used to describe as "becoming the asshole." You spend your whole career bitching about the assholes at the top, and then one day you realize that you *are* the asshole at the top. Sometimes the decisions you have to make as a business owner are agonizingly difficult. Sometimes you can get sidetracked into the most expedient, efficient solution and miss your chance to do the right thing. Or you might get caught in an endless internal debate of what's right for the business versus what's right for the individuals involved. Many times, you'll struggle to do what is right—often at tremendous financial risk and personal cost—and then get zero credit for it from the people you are trying so hard to lead.

Nonetheless, it's easier to lead your company into being a company you're proud of if you operate with steadfast guiding principles—the things that you stick to regardless of stress levels, time crunches, or monetary cost. As they say, a principle is not a principle until it costs you money.

Creating a company gives you a chance to play a larger part in the world. A company—any company—becomes a distinct and separate entity of its own, reaching beyond the personality, energy, and limitations of its founder. With your own company, you have a chance to add to the world. This could be in the sense of:

- Giving back to your community by funding and promoting good works
- Doing your daily work in an ethical and socially responsible way
- Treating your customers and clients fairly and honestly
- Supporting your employees in building balanced lives as well as interesting careers
- Providing products or services of the highest quality and integrity

It's a question worth some thought: In what ways can your company best add to the world?

One of the primary benefits of approaching your business in this way is that when you wake up in the middle of the night wondering why the hell you work so hard, you can offer yourself some meaningful reasons beyond money and force of habit. This approach can also add fresh inspiration to your days even when the menial tasks of your chosen profession have lost the challenge they once held for you.

If you're trying to divine your own company's values and principles, it sometimes helps to think of them in terms of concentric circles, starting with yourself in the middle and the world at large in the outer-most circle. What do you believe is your company's responsibility to you, to your employees (or even your family), to your clients or customers, to your vendors and support companies, to your local community, to your industry, and to your world?

As long as you're the one making the big decisions, you might want to consider the bigger picture as well. From Starbucks to UPS, you'll find many larger companies now evaluating, strategizing, and promoting their success at being a corporate citizen. Just as one person who recycles can make a difference, so can one small business that considers its impact on the world. Do you feel a sense of responsibility, or even a faint stirring of excitement, at the thought of your company becoming a role model for social responsibility and sustainability? Do you care how your company will affect the planet environmentally? Economically? Socially? In what positive ways can your business influence and shape those inside and outside of your company? As Gandhi said, "You must be the change you wish to see in the world."

PT&Co.: Great Work, Great Workplace, Great Communities That Work

The leaders at PT&Co. manage with three clearly defined goals as guiding principles:

1. They focus on creating outstanding work, which is what attracts their clients and keeps them there.
2. They strive to create a supportive workplace to attract and retain the sort of star talent that can produce excellent work for clients.
3. They do what they can to help create healthy, sustainable communities.

"For me, my management philosophy is the golden rule," Patrice says. "You treat people the way you want them to treat you. That can be the guiding principle for how you run any endeavor, whether it's a business or a volunteer organization."

For many years Patrice says she thought that attracting clients and keeping them were the two pillars her company should stand on. More recently, they added a third pillar to their foundation. "We want our work and energy to be applied appropriately to clients who contribute to the community in positive ways. We've got to feel that we're creating great communities that work."

PT&Co. has a matrix they use to evaluate potential clients for an appropriate fit with their guiding principles. The sweet spot of the matrix is the intersection between being able to do strong work and contributing to the world in a positive way. If a client falls into the wrong quadrant of the matrix, the agency won't take them on. "For instance, we've been approached over the years by three different tobacco manufacturers," says Patrice. "There's no way we can justify working for a tobacco company, even for an arm of the company that has nothing to do with tobacco."

The agency also puts its money where its mouth is when they are faced with a client that doesn't treat agency staffers well. In fact, they once resigned their biggest account because of the impact it was having on employees. "Their product was perfectly good and necessary," remembers Patrice. "But the clients themselves were abusive. We addressed it and it wasn't changing." The reaction within the agency ranged from celebration and pride to anxiety about potential layoffs. The partners had considered the financial implications before resigning the account, however, so all agency jobs were safe. The partners did forfeit any raises for themselves and the agency squeaked through that year without turning a profit.

PT&Co. also resigned a large client that had taken an anti-gay position in the face of a publicity fiasco. "They were in a crisis situation,"

Patrice says. "We needed to help them through the crisis, so we did, but ultimately we had to resign the account because we couldn't in good conscience support their point of view."

Patrice feels that taking a stand on issues this way may have cost them some profit occasionally, but doesn't see how her company could have responded otherwise. "Over the years, it hasn't been easy," she says. "Our growth has been erratic at times because we've taken strong positions. But in one respect, a lot of people in our industry know who we are because we stand for something." Some would challenge Patrice on her position. But for that she has a philosophical response: "I see it in terms of the butterfly effect. Our actions here in this room have far-reaching ramifications. The beating of a butterfly's wings in the rain forest of Brazil can create changes in the weather on the other side of the world." She acknowledges that buy-in to this view varies, even among workers at her company.

Patrice speaks of community in the largest sense of the word—not just her workplace or industry, but our world. "I believe we are all one," she says. "Everyone who lives on this planet is connected." Every year on Valentine's Day, PT&Co. closes to give everybody in the company a day to go out and commit what they term "acts of love and kindness." Employees volunteer all over the city, from soup-kitchen shifts to park cleanups to meal deliveries for those homebound by HIV/AIDS. When they presented their Valentine's Day concept to the New York Chapter of the Public Relations Society of America with the goal of expanding its reach, the idea was enthusiastically embraced. Now more than sixty public relations agencies and other corporate communications companies celebrate Valentine's Day with random acts of love and kindness throughout the city.

KooKoo Bear Kids:
Treat Your Customers like Your Friends

Not all business owners take such an extreme big-picture view of their effect on the world as Patrice does. Others, like Tara, focus on their more immediate community: customers and their kids. Tara is empathetic toward her customers and what they're dealing with as mothers because that life is her life too. "My big thing is to treat the customer like your friend," she says. "If there's a problem with a product, or someone wants to return something, I want the employees on the phone to offer right away to refund their money. My training is that the customer is never wrong."

Although Tara gives her employees free rein in many areas, she keeps an ear out for how customers are being treated on the phone. "I don't want my employees ever yelling at a customer," she says. "If I hear someone getting snippy, I'll run out of my office and say, 'Stop, slow down. Put her on hold. I'll get someone else to help her.'"

This doesn't mean that customers never yell at the customer service reps. "That happens a lot," Tara says. "You get someone screaming at you and you have to be understanding. Maybe the customer's baby had a hard, bad day and she was up all night. But do you know how hard it was to get that customer to call us? How much money it cost to get that phone to ring?" There's a clear business reason for treating that customer as a friend.

Relationships are key to every part of Tara's business, not just with her customers but also with her husband and sister, vendors, and employees. She considers all of them friends and doesn't treat business relationships any differently from her personal friendships. Her employees typically come to her through friends of friends, and Tara soon considers them friends as well. This is one of the reasons she has so much difficulty firing anyone. Her husband Joe generally sits with her during those sorts of conversations because she feels she needs his support. "My husband is from a very structured environment," she says, "but I'm more casual about things."

Tara has initiated a relationship with CureSearch, a charity for childhood cancer research, partly because two children in her sons' school are dealing with cancer. "I wanted to give something back," Tara said. "I wanted a charity for KooKoo Bear Kids and this one felt perfect."

Tara also used Tom Glavine, a major league baseball player, and his family as models in her catalog, and donates a percentage of the proceeds from the clothing they're pictured wearing. Glavine (formerly of the Atlanta Braves) pitches for the New York Mets, and serves as official spokesperson for CureSearch.

Kids are what KooKoo Bear is all about. Another of Tara's guiding principles is to resist any pressure to separate work and family into two distinctly separate areas of her life. In the early years, she once hired a photographer who expected to have everything meticulously prepared for him ahead of time and to be working in a purely professional environment. "He showed up and was like, why are there children here?" says Tara. "And I said, those are my kids. My new photographer brings his own kids to the photo shoots. That's a big part of it to me. You can have the kids right in the middle of it all. I think that's why it works."

Financial Stress Reduction:
For the Love of Money, Fun, and Doing Good

Chellie Campbell's entire business is based on teaching people new guiding principles about money. Her workshops, lectures, and writing are all focused on helping people shift old thinking about financial issues, so they can make more money and have more time off for fun. It's not surprising, then, that her personal guiding principles reflect that same thinking.

"I have three guiding principles," Chellie says. "Everything I do needs to be a lot of fun, make a lot of money, and do a lot of good. I look at everything proposed to me with those three goals in mind. Sometimes I'll say yes to something that will do a lot of good and be a lot of fun but not make a lot of money, but I prefer to have all three."

She also does a conscious screening to determine the people she's going to do business with. She describes three kinds of people, whom she refers to as dolphins, sharks, and tunas. Dolphins are intelligent and fun-loving. Sharks are eating machines; it's their job to eat everything. Tunas are the complainers, the victims of the sharks.

"So what you want to do," she says, "is find dolphins to swim with and do business with and avoid the shark and tuna. Because sharks are going to steal your money and tuna are going to leech from you by wasting your time."

This leads to another of Chellie's guiding principles: It's okay (in fact it's wonderful) to have a lot of money. She urges her students to promote peace and prosperity for all, but to start with having it themselves.

Earlier in life, when Chellie was beginning to explore metaphysical thinking, she noticed that the spiritually minded people she was meeting and reading about seemed to consider money a bad thing. "I think we're supposed to learn how to use [money] for everybody's benefit," she says. "How does it serve anybody for spiritual people to be broke? To me, that just didn't make any sense."

Chellie is guided by the idea that money is not a necessary evil, but just plain necessary. "Money is a flow," she says. "It comes in; it goes out. You just get to direct the flow. And so, what you want to do is get the most coming in so that you can send the most out with blessings. Use it with love."

She counsels people to give with joy and be happy both about the bills they pay and the money they're able to give away. "People so often relate spending or giving money with fear. You have to start trusting

instant wisdom

ON GUIDING PRINCIPLES

Owning a company allows you the opportunity to play large. How can your company add to the world?

Guiding principles for your company are not just about making the world a better place. Start with how your company could make your own life better.

Doing the right thing and being popular are sometimes mutually exclusive. Get over it.

Even a small company has an impact on the world. Whether it's positive or negative is up to the ones who run it.

Your guiding principles don't necessarily need to involve grand gestures. Some of the most powerful guiding principles are expressed in the smallest of actions, like rectifying an honest mistake or offering a kind word when it's needed most.

that you will get more. Start trusting in your ability to do that. And get off of this fear and start being about love and service and fun and happiness. You want to get some more [money] because then you can do more with it."

To help counteract old fears and past miseducation about money, Chellie prescribes positive thinking through the method of affirmations. She uses affirmations herself daily and says that's key. "Everybody knows what positive thinking is. Every self-help book on the planet talks about it," she says. "But [most people] are not actively practicing it. Just knowing about exercise and diet doesn't make you thinner. You still have to go to the gym, not just lie around the spa and get a massage." Chellie verbalizes her affirmations daily, working them into her morning routine.

"I do them after I get dressed and put my makeup on," she says. "Before I sit down at the computer, before I make a phone call, I make sure I get myself in the mood for all that."

Chellie offers a few examples of her affirmations: "People love to give me money. That's my number one affirmation. Another one is, I receive large sums of money just for being me. You know, that's happened to me before. People read my book and decide to tithe to me."

Another key principle for Chellie is keeping herself undercommitted, which some might say is counterintuitive to success. But Chellie feels it's of primary importance to her ability to do well in business. "I used to be one of the overcommitters," she says. "When they asked me to run for president of yet another networking group, I said no and they asked me why. It was because I finally figured out that I've been president of every club I've ever belonged to since I was twelve."

Chellie feels she can't be at her best if she's exhausted or if her days are filled to the brim with activity. "You don't have creative ideas in the middle of your busy day when you're running down your to-do list that is four pages long," she says. "Creative ideas come when you're at rest."

This leads to the guiding principle that seems to be the buttress of everything about Chellie and her business. "I have a different model of business," she says. "I live life my own way." ■

✂️ **ALICE GOLDSMITH** is the owner of Alice Goldsmith Ceramics in New York City, founded in 1997. She handcrafts porcelain dinnerware and accessories and sells them to high-end retailers.

How did you know it was time to start your own company?
It just made sense. It looked terrible on paper, but it made sense. I'd had several different careers, but I never found anything that could hold my interest before.

Did it feel like a big risk?
When I signed my New York City lease, it felt serious.

How much startup capital did it take?
Not enough. More than I had available.

Did you have a formal business plan laid out?
Not one that anybody would recognize as such.

How long was it until you could pay yourself?
I just started giving myself a weekly paycheck about a year ago. That doesn't mean I cash them every week, though. Before, I used to just write myself a check when I needed it.

Before you started your company what were you clueless about?
Ceramic technique.

How do you find customers?
I do trade shows and also [work] by referral.

What's your finest wisdom on developing new business?
You know, I usually have a number in my head of the numbers I want to make for a month or a year. And somehow it just happens. There's a lot of faith involved. It's weird that way.

What's the best advice anybody ever gave you?
Trust and everything will come out okay.

What's one mistake you won't make twice?
Starting a company with no resources at all. All I had was an idea. I did it by the seat of my pants.

What couldn't you have done without?
The willingness to risk failure. It was a series of small steps. The worst-case scenario was that I'd have learned something new and I'd have a lot of Christmas gifts to give away.

What do you like best about owning your own company?
The people who cross my path.

What do you like least?
The lack of balance between work and leisure.

Describe your best day and your worst day.
My best day is when everything happens the way it's supposed to. Everything runs smoothly. I get to exercise. My crew is happy. My glaze kiln fires. Everything just works. My worst day is the reverse. The kiln breaks. I can't go to the gym and everyone's having a hissy fit in the studio.

What's the secret to making it work?
When you're on the right path, the doors just open for you. It's not like it's not a lot of hard work, but the right people just appear. Someone would offer to take my work around, someone who didn't even know me. Another person gave me the keys to their studio and let me fire in their kiln. It really happened through the generosity of strangers.

Could you ever work for someone else again?
Sure, I'd probably make a better employee now. I'd appreciate it a lot more. I do like having my own thing, though. It's an amazing thing to see what I've accomplished. It's been an incredible experience.

How would a guy run your business differently?
He probably wouldn't take as much shit from his employees. Maybe he wouldn't be as intuitive. When things go wrong, I don't really go crazy

about it. Actually, in a ceramics studio, a man would probably run it pretty much the same. Maybe he wouldn't cry.

❦ **BARBARA HERRICK** is the owner of Scandia Down Shop in Jackson Hole, Wyoming. Her company is a retailer of high-end furnishings, known for down products and bedding.

How did you know it was time to start your own business?
I was young enough to believe I had nothing to lose.

Did it feel like a big risk?
Yes.

How much startup capital did it take?
More than $100,000.

How long was it before you could pay yourself?
Right off.

Who are your role models?
Successful women business owners.

What would you tell a friend whose business is growing faster than she can handle?
Re-evaluate your plan for success and decide whether it is really worth getting bigger.

What's the best advice anybody ever gave you?
Give it all you have.

What's one mistake you won't make twice?
Not going with my gut feelings.

What couldn't you have done without?
The support from my family and working 24/7.

Does having your own business give you more or less freedom than working for someone else?
At first, less. Now, much more.

Describe your best day and your worst day.
Busy day. Slow day.

How has having your own business affected your marriage?
My husband has to help more—especially with our child.

What does your child think about what you do?
Loves it.

How would a guy run your business differently?
He'd probably be more numbers oriented.

🏃 **JENNIFER POUNDS** is president of Frog: The Atlanta-Paris Connection (*www.frogapc.com*). Her company offers French immersion trips to France, private tours of France, French lessons and translation, and interpretation services.

How did you know it was time to start your own company?
I was tired of working for someone else, of having to deal with corporate politics, boring meetings, and backstabbing coworkers. The final straw was having only two weeks' vacation. I figured that if I worked for myself, I could take as long a vacation as I wanted, when I wanted!

Did it feel like a big risk?
I tend to be a risk-taker and for me, part of that is being somewhat clueless about just how big a leap I'm about to take.

How much startup capital did it take?
I started with very little, a couple of thousand dollars perhaps.

How long until you were able to pay yourself?
I didn't pay myself a true salary until the fifth year in business, but I took distributions before that.

Did you have a formal business plan laid out?
No.

Before you started your company, what were you clueless about?
How to run a business—the basics like taxes, which ones to pay, when to pay, how to pay, what not to pay, why it's better to wait to pay some things; and also how best to market oneself and one's company. I'm still not sure that I'm exhausting all those possibilities.

How do you find customers?
Mostly by word of mouth and through the local university (Emory) where I teach continuing education classes. More and more, people find me on the Internet in Google searches which lead them to my Web site.

What's your finest wisdom on developing new business?
Be open and expect it to come.

What's the secret to a successful cash flow?
I plan ahead, writing out checks that have to be sent several months later when I have the money in the account.

How did you know it was time to hire your first employee?
I still haven't done that.

What do you tell yourself during slow times?
There is a wonderful proverb in French that says, "Bit by bit, the bird builds its nest." This is possibly the best advice I've ever heard.

What would you tell a friend whose company is going through a dry spell?
Spend the time brainstorming and, if possible, take a vacation or do something else that you love. Ideas come when you're in a good place, when you're happy and surrounded by people and things you love.

What would you tell someone whose business is growing faster than she can handle?
Slow down and take it one step at a time. I'd rather say no to a client than to do work that I'm not proud of.

What's one mistake you won't make twice?

Making a mistake on an invoice for a client who was not understanding and wouldn't accept the corrected invoice. Needless to say, this was the last time I worked for her!

What do you like best about owning your own company?

I love that it's mine—all mine! I can do what I want, when I want, how I want, wearing what I want (OK, most of the time I can do this, I still have to take my clients into account!). What's good and works comes from me, with lots of help from friends; and what doesn't work is also mine and gives me opportunities to learn.

What do you like least?

Taxes. Hiring a good accountant is one of the best things I've done. It also feels lonely sometimes.

What couldn't you have done without?

Working with a career coach, being surrounded by people who believed in me and disliking the corporate job I had.

Does your business improve your lifestyle or make your life more difficult?

After seven years in business, it has improved my lifestyle. At first it was difficult for me to manage my time and I still have moments when I'm not as efficient as I would like to be.

Does having your own business give you more or less freedom than working for someone else?

Definitely more.

Could you ever work for someone else again?

I suppose that I could, but I don't think that I would be as happy as I am now. It would be nice to finish work, leave, and not worry about anything until the next time I returned to work.

What do you think you'll do next?

I plan to divide my time between France and Atlanta. I'll continue my business as it is, but hopefully have more time to explore some artistic desires I've had for a while.

How would a guy run your business differently?

I suppose that he might be more aggressive than I am—at least the advice I've had from men friends has always felt a bit aggressive to me.

MILLIE GRENOUGH is president of Grenough LLC (*www.grenough.com*), located in New Haven, Connecticut. Millie is a motivational speaker, coach, consultant, and trainer dedicated to helping people reach their full potential. Her training and experience converge in a unique blend of state-of-the-art techniques in stress management, performance coaching, and life skills enhancement.

How did you know it was time to start your own business?

When I got bored with what I was doing and knew that I wanted to do more, and have autonomy doing it.

Did it feel like a big risk?

No, it just felt like the next step.

How much startup capital did it take?

About $30,000. I was already paying mortgage on an office condo; moved my business into that.

Did you have a formal business plan laid out?

Not a well-laid-out one. More like following my instincts.

How long was it until you could pay yourself?

About two years.

Before you started your company, what were you clueless about?

How many new things I'd have to learn.

How do you find clients?
Mainly through satisfied customers and through relationships.

What's your finest wisdom on how to gain new business?
Be yourself. Do excellent work. Respect yourself and every one you come in contact with.

What's the secret to a successful cash flow?
Good work + good bookkeeping.

How did you know it was time to hire your first employee?
When I was feeling overloaded with things I didn't want to do.

How do you motivate or inspire your employees?
By inviting them to inspire me, too.

What's the most difficult thing about managing employees?
By my own choice, my business is small. I have several part-time employees. Most difficult thing is synchronizing my high-demand times with their schedules.

Who are your role models?
Gloria Steinem, Hillary Clinton, Roya Hakakian, Aung San Suu Kyi (the Burmese leader, Nobel Prize winner).

What do you tell yourself during slow times?
Remember that these times have happened before and I have gotten through them. It's part of the rhythm. Give myself a break and do something I like now instead of getting depressed.

What would you tell a friend whose company is going through a dry spell?
Everything has seasons. Tulip bulbs are under the ground for many months before they show their colors—but that doesn't mean they're dead.

What would you tell someone whose business is growing faster than she can handle?
Pause. Look at the big picture; see what you really want.

What's the best advice anybody ever gave you?
[To] ask myself: What shines for you? Then follow that light.

What's one mistake you won't make twice?
Follow someone else's advice just because I think they must know more than I do.

What couldn't you have done without?
The emotional support of my family and friends, plus my own bull-headed determination.

What do you like best about owning your own company?
Creating what I want to create.

What do you like least?
Taking care of so many details.

Describe your best day and your worst day.
Best day: I'm doing interactive presentations or working with motivated individuals or groups to help them go after what they want. Worst day: I have tons of e-mail and phone calls to respond to and very little time for rest or for doing stimulating things with others.

Does your business improve your lifestyle or make your life more difficult?
It improves my lifestyle in that I meet all kinds of people, go to interesting places, and do unusual things. It's more difficult in that I haven't yet mastered the art of practicing what I preach about life/work balance.

Does having your own business give you more or less freedom than working for someone else?
More emotional freedom. Less spare time.

How has having your own business affected your marriage?
I think [owning my own business has] added spice to my marriage. My husband has his own small business. We help each other out with challenges, and celebrate our successes.

What do your kids think about what you do?
I think they actually look to their dad and me as pretty fine role models. They know that we haven't taken the usual route. They also know that we're not making tons of money because of our choices. They get it that "security" isn't as important to us as doing what we think we're good at doing and enjoy doing, and giving that back to the world.

Could you ever work for someone else again?
Not work for. Possibly work with, if I was really excited about the person and what he or she was doing.

What do you think you'll do next?
Finish writing my next book, take it on the road, and then begin another one.

Do you have an exit plan?
Not really well defined. Work fairly full-time till I'm seventy; begin tapering down now to focus on what I really like doing and let some other things go. Living off my royalties and continuing to do presentations would be enjoyable.

How would a guy run your business differently?
He'd probably have a much more formalized business plan and be guided much more by bottom line figures. (Maybe I could learn something from him!) ∎

Please know that I am aware of the hazards.
I want to do it because I want to do it.

Amelia Earhart

❧

3

The Labor Pains of a Successful Startup

—

Just as with having babies, the birth of every startup is different. Some start-ups involve pain and suffering, and long stretches where you think you just can't take it for another second. Others are relatively painless—in ret-rospect, at least. If you're feeling hesitant about starting your own com-pany because you're not convinced you know what you're doing, bear in mind that you've got plenty of company. Many women entrepreneurs say that they had no idea what they were getting into when they launched their businesses. On the other hand, many entrepreneurs (and most of the women in this book) say that starting their own company was one of the single best things they've ever done for themselves, and they have a difficult time imagining ever working for someone else again.

The startup phase, regardless of the difficulties, is generally recalled with the misty romanticism of falling in love. There's an intensity to the early days that makes you feel very much alive. Colors are brighter, jokes are funnier, and days are longer than twenty-four hours (how else could you possibly have gotten all that done with little to no help?). Although most entrepreneurs work pretty darn hard during the startup phase, almost every one of them remembers that stretch as being a hell of a lot of fun.

When my friend B.A. Albert and I started MATCH, my first ad agency, we'd spend all day answering phone calls and going to client meetings, and then use the evenings for our real work. The lamplight would glow against the brick walls of our warehouse office and an occasional train would rumble by outside. We shared a gigantic borrowed dining table for our desk, where we'd sit across from each other laughing and talking and thinking up ideas for ads until we were so weary we were on the point of tears. Then we'd pushpin our best ideas to the wall and sit back and feel proud of what we were building. What we were doing wasn't easy, but it was immensely satisfying.

For my second ad agency, the startup process really didn't involve much besides printing some letterhead and calling my corporate attorney to file the articles of incorporation. I set up shop in a sunny home studio built off my kitchen and Tribe was in business.

In turn, each of the women below had her own unique experience of bringing a company into the world. Some were more difficult births than others; all are remembered with joyful pride.

PT&Co.:
Buying Your Freedom

Patrice Tanaka is not the kind of person who grew up wanting to start a business. She says, "I consider myself an accidental entrepreneur." Patrice was raised on an island of Hawaii, in a community small enough that everybody knew each other. She moved to New York for a career in public relations, and ended up working with a partner who could have put Heather Locklear's character from *Melrose Place* to shame. Patrice remembers that a colleague once described her former partner by saying, "Her skirt's so short, you can see her balls." This first partner ended up selling the small PR firm to Chiat/Day, one of the leading advertising agencies in the country and eventually left the business. Patrice was left to run things under the new parent company.

"We were a very creative agency," Patrice says. "And then suddenly we were part of Chiat/Day, and they were like, 'Why do you need creativity in PR? Why did Jay [Chiat] acquire them?' They had no concept of what we did."

Meanwhile, the business climate was moving steadily from the go-go 1980s to the more sobering 1990s. Patrice began to worry that her parent company would shut down her firm if the economy continued its decline. She gathered together the key people at her agency and voiced her concerns.

Patrice had a vague idea that they could buy themselves back from Chiat/Day, but she had no clue as to the logistics of how such a buyback would work. "I'm not such a business-savvy kind of person," she says. "Everything we did in terms of starting the agency was kind of intuitive because I hadn't read business books. Why would I? I wasn't interested in starting a business before."

The motivation for the buyout wasn't about money; it was about being able to control the ability to continue working as a team. So Patrice spent a long stretch of time trying to build consensus among the team members. "We sat together for several months talking. Finally, I said as long as I have six out of twelve people on board, plus me as the seventh, that's a majority. I could go to Jay and ask if we could buy ourselves back."

Patrice planned her approach to Jay Chiat carefully. She decided to wait to call him until he would be offsite in Aspen, where she knew he would be relaxed and, she hoped, agreeable. She called him a number of times before she got a return call. Finally, he called her back, and Patrice laid out her case.

"I said, 'Jay, we're concerned that given what might happen in the economy, you guys might not be interested in continuing to have a PR subsidiary. So frankly, we feel it might be better for us to be more in control of our future. What we want to do is buy ourselves back and be independent again, just like we were.'"

Her heartfelt and well-rehearsed speech was met with dead silence. After a very long moment, Jay Chiat said, "Well, if you're telling me that you all want to do this, then we'll have to make some accommodation for that."

Patrice started gushing in relief and gratitude. The phone clicked and that was the end of the discussion. "He wasn't about to elaborate," says Patrice. The next phone call she got was from the acquisitions person at Chiat/Day. He didn't even say hello, just, "Patrice? We want a million dollars."

Patrice and her group didn't have a million dollars. "I think we met with seven banks," she says. "I remember the person from Citibank saying, 'What is a PR agency?' And I thought, Oh my God, we're screwed."

Patrice's lawyer urged her to think of something he could use in negotiation. It turned out that the combined Chiat/Day stock Patrice and two colleagues owned would eventually have been worth about $375,000, so the lawyer was able to negotiate the deal based on Chiat/Day not having to pay that money out. In the end, Patrice and her partners were able to buy themselves back at a dramatically lower price than Chiat/Day's initial request. "So we paid very little down and a royalty fee on our income for the next three years," Patrice says.

With that, PT&Co. was off and running—sort of. "We took the clients that we had. But we didn't have office space, furniture, or equipment. We had no track record for the company. We didn't have a bank or cash reserves. All we had was the operating income from the current clients." Patrice Tanaka had officially joined the ranks of entrepreneurs.

KooKoo Bear Kids:
Buying Lots of Stuff and Piling It in the Basement

Tara's background before KooKoo Bear Kids—and before having her own kids—was first in the retail business and then in wholesale. She was a buyer in New York with Saks Fifth Avenue and then moved over to 7th Avenue to work for the dress designer Victor Costa, a designer known for the sort of lavish gowns that you might have seen on *Dynasty* or Ivana Trump. Tara spent the next handful of years traveling all over for her accounts and to shows.

She and her husband, Joe, eventually ended up in Atlanta. Joe started a software company in his off hours, and when Tara got pregnant, she quit working to help him launch the company. "We started it in our apartment, literally," Tara says. Joe began to attract investors, and eventually sold his controlling shares and stepped out.

After that, Joe was able to stay home and help Tara with the kids for a year or two, occasionally dabbling in some real estate and building projects on Hilton Head. When he got an offer for a job in California, Tara nixed the idea. "I didn't want to leave Atlanta," she says. "The kids were settled. I'd gotten my first son into school. It was tough to get him in. I wanted to stay here."

They started tossing around ideas of what they might do with their careers in Atlanta. Having weathered one startup together, they knew they were a good business team. "I said, let's do something with kids," remembers Tara. "I was really focused on baby gifts in the beginning."

Tara continued to brainstorm, sharing her ideas with Joe as they developed, until they agreed on the niche of high-end babies' and children's gifts and furnishings. Originally, she was thinking of a retail store, but Joe was concerned that a store wouldn't make enough money so he suggested the idea of a catalog and associated Web site.

Tara named the catalog and Web site after her middle son, Connor, who was nicknamed Coo-Coo Bear as a baby. She and Joe first considered a French word for the company name, then Italian. They had been casting about for a name that would be more personal, and one day when the whole extended family was sitting on the beach, someone suggested Connor's nickname. Nowadays, when people hear Connor being called by his pet name, they often ask Tara what prompted her to name her child after a catalog.

Tara started scouting items and grew more excited. "We realized there really wasn't anything out there in the high-end market, not with the sort of specialty items I wanted to offer," says Tara. Joe trusted her judgment and agreed to back the company financially. Tara remembers him saying, "Listen, if you want to do this, go start. Go start buying stuff." So Tara began shopping with a vengeance, and the basement started to fill up with boxes and boxes of comforters and pillows, beds and bookcases, gift items, and tchotchkes.

Soon the merchandise began to take over more than the basement. Photo shoots for the catalog were staged all over the house. "I had beds being shot in the kitchen, so that was a big disruption," Tara says. They used their own sons and neighbors' children as models. "I'd grab kids wherever I could. And we'd say, see that bed? Go jump on that bed." Tara's style is definitely unfussy, and she wanted her catalog to feel that way too. She let the kids in the shots do what kids do naturally rather than have them styled and posed. "When we were shooting, we'd work from eight in the morning until late at night because it takes a lot of time to get one shot," Tara remembers. "It was wild. There were times when I thought, what am I doing? But it was a blast."

Tara's sister Trace, a veteran of a leading furnishings catalog, gave her a quick education in the catalog business and was able to help after-hours, but she still had a full-time job to go to every morning. Joe was handling all the financial details of the business. Tara began to feel the pressure of everything else that would fall onto her shoulders. "How am I going to do this?" she remembers thinking. "I've got three kids."

Tara had an office off her kitchen with a door she could shut for phone calls without hearing kids going crazy in the background. But for the most part, she didn't draw a line between her family life and her business life. "My kids were very involved in the business," she says. "They had to be. I don't think you can tell small children, 'Listen, this is Mommy's job now. She has been a full-time mother and stayed home with you and now she's jumped to the other side.'"

Trace hooked Tara up with a talented freelance copywriter to write the catalog. Tara remembers his shock when he arrived at the bedlam that was her house: "He's tripping all over comforters and pillows; the dog's barking, the kids are running around," Tara remembers. "He said, 'Do you have all the product information?' And I said, 'Oh yeah, I can fill it out.' He said, 'No, no, your vendors need to give you the complete information.' It was clear I had never done this before." The copywriter persevered, despite the noise level and other challenges, and eventually the catalog began to take shape.

At last, the first catalog was printed and sent in the mail to their rudimentary beginnings of a database. The mailing list was expensive and not specifically targeted to catalog buyers, but it was what they could get their hands on at the time. Tara and Joe waited anxiously for the phones to ring. When they still hadn't received the first call after twelve days, Tara was reaching a state of panic about the amount of money they'd dumped into the catalog. "I was like, 'We're dead,'" she says. Finally, the orders began trickling in. They were taking orders during the day and shipping at night as the phone began to ring more and more. "No one worked for us then," Tara says. "It was just Trace and Joe and me—all so tired, we couldn't see straight. It was hysterical, absolutely hysterical." In spite of Tara's initial fears, KooKoo Bear Kids was not dead at all. It was alive and adamantly kicking.

Financial Stress Reduction:
Buying into Her Dream

Chellie Campbell is considered by her many fans to be a guru of enlightened money management. She works as a workshop leader and speaker on financial stress reduction, and is writing her second book on a spiritual approach to wealth.

Chellie once ran a bookkeeping service owned by two attorneys. "It was basically one person and a computer," Chellie says. "That person left, and the lawyers hired me to come in and make something of it."

At the end of the first year, they gave Chellie 20 percent ownership in the bookkeeping company in lieu of a holiday bonus. "That's when the entrepreneurial light bulb went off for me," says Chellie. "I had never thought about owning a business. I sort of turned the company around and made nice with all the clients who had been mad." By the end of the first year, Chellie had added three more employees and had won new clients. Over the next four years her company grew from $80,000 to $420,000 a year in sales.

Chellie enjoyed that feeling of success but is quick to temper it now. "It was the 1980s," she says. "I heard Jon Goodman, who was the chair of the University of Southern California economics department, give a speech and she said, 'Any idiot could make money in the eighties.'"

In January of 1988, Chellie bought out the lawyers' interest in the company. "I was doing all the work," she says. "I wanted to own it myself."

Near-disaster struck when she suddenly lost the company's biggest account with almost no warning. As she tried to rebuild her business, she dug herself deeper and deeper into debt. After a long and costly struggle, she finally managed to save the company.

Chellie noticed that small business clients and friends all around her were suffering as well. "It was the end of 1989 and the recession had hit California. People starting calling out of the blue to ask me to lunch," she says. "They all brought a pad of paper and a pencil with them and they said something like, 'You were in trouble last year. I'm in trouble now. What did you do?' I started giving advice over lunch and three people in the same week said, 'Chellie, you should teach this.'"

Another entrepreneurial light bulb went off for Chellie. A few years earlier, she had attended a seminar led by a man named Roger Lane. She was so impressed with his material, which focused not on saving money but making more of it, that she contacted him to ask if he would teach a class in her area if she pulled enough friends together. He agreed, and she was able to sign up fifty people for the class. Roger then asked Chellie if she would produce him in Los Angeles, and that's how she got her training in running workshops, while simultaneously running her own bookkeeping business.

When her friends suggested she teach some of what she knew, Chellie already had the mechanics of the workshop business model under her belt.

Chellie set out to market her workshop by mailing a flyer to all her contacts and then following up by phone. She convinced a dozen people to sign up and then got busy writing the material. This was the beginning of Chellie's financial stress reduction workshop career.

Chellie taught the workshops on the side for four years while rebuilding her bookkeeping service. Eventually, her evening workshop students challenged her to make a change because she was burning herself out doing both. "I was just getting exhausted," she says. "The workshops were my passion. I saw people change and get better and make more money right in front of me in sixty days. I was teaching everybody in my

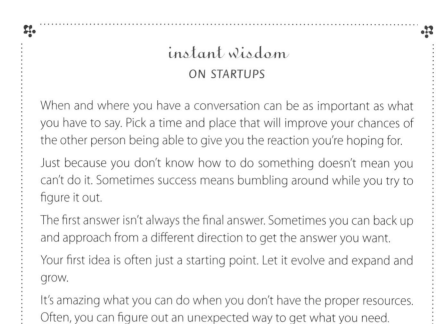

instant wisdom
ON STARTUPS

When and where you have a conversation can be as important as what you have to say. Pick a time and place that will improve your chances of the other person being able to give you the reaction you're hoping for.

Just because you don't know how to do something doesn't mean you can't do it. Sometimes success means bumbling around while you try to figure it out.

The first answer isn't always the final answer. Sometimes you can back up and approach from a different direction to get the answer you want.

Your first idea is often just a starting point. Let it evolve and expand and grow.

It's amazing what you can do when you don't have the proper resources. Often, you can figure out an unexpected way to get what you need.

Following your dream will feel like the right decision. When you know it, you know it.

class to go for it and do their dream picture and create their life the way they wanted it to be. I was afraid to let go of the regular money. The more I looked at it, the more I said I have to go for it." Chellie wasn't sure if she could make enough money teaching workshops, but she felt she had to try. And of course, it turned out that Chellie was in fact able to make a living teaching workshops—a most handsome living indeed. ∎

🐾 **DR. MICHELLE TILGHMAN** is a veterinarian and CEO of the Loving Touch Animal Center (*www.lovingtouchac.com*) in Stone Mountain, Georgia. The center combines classical and complementary medicine and has evolved to become a training facility for veterinary students and veterinarians.

What were you doing before you started your company?
I was working in Texas for another holistic practitioner before I moved here. I showed up in Stone Mountain with an abusive husband, a baby, a horse, some goats, a dog, and a bird. But I also had an acupuncture kit and my microscope.

Did it feel like a big risk?
No.

How much startup capital did it take?
I went in to see this woman banker and actually had my baby with me at the time. She gave me a $10,000 loan.

Did you have a formal business plan laid out?
Yes.

How do you find clients?
Word of mouth.

What do you do for marketing?
Seek out like-minded people and do presentations or speaking engagements.

What's the secret to a successful cash flow?
Keep tabs on money daily.

How did you know it was time to hire your first employee?
I couldn't do surgery and answer the phone at the same time.

What's the secret to hiring the right people?
Make sure their hearts are in the right place.

How do you motivate or inspire your employees?
By having honesty and setting an example.

What's the most difficult thing about managing employees?
Realizing that they do not necessarily have a personal interest in the business.

How do you know you have to fire someone?
When they do things totally against your mission statement.

What do you tell yourself during slow times?
It will get better.

What would you tell a friend whose business was going through a slow time?
Do meditation to bring in business.

Whom do you talk to when you need advice or a sounding board?
My husband, David. (David is not the abusive one I moved here with—I got rid of him.)

What's the best advice anybody ever gave you?
Take care of yourself, because nobody else will.

What couldn't you have done without?
The drive that I had to do the right medicine for the animals.

What do you like best about owning your own company?
The ability to have a healthy workplace, run with compassion.

Does your business improve your lifestyle or make your life more difficult?
It has improved [my life] by giving me a good income, but it [has also given] me increased responsibility.

How has having your own business affected your relationships?
I [have] had to learn to balance things so that I make my marriage and family number one and my business number two.

What do your kids think about what you do?
They love it and hate it. But overall, it's provided them with a great place to grow up. They've had a village.

Could you ever work for someone else again?
No.

What do you think you'll do next?
Teach.

How would a guy run your business differently?
It wouldn't be the Loving Touch.

JULIE JACOBS is the managing partner of York Solutions in Westchester, Illinois. Her company, started in 1989, is a direct hire, contract, and temporary solutions firm based in the Chicago area.

How did you know it was time to start your own company?
I knew I couldn't afford to do what I wanted on someone else's wages.

Did it feel like a big risk?
Not really. I didn't look at it that way.

How much startup capital did it take?
I had a partner who put in $100,000. He stayed at his job and I worked for free in the beginning.

How long was it before you could pay yourself?
Six months.

How do you find your clients?
Networking.

What's your finest wisdom on developing new business?
Be honest. And deliver the goods.

How did you know it was time to hire your first employee?
I was working seventy hours a week and I could afford to hire someone.

What's the secret to hiring the right people?
Make it a slow process.

How do you know when it's time to fire someone?
You don't enjoy seeing [the person] or you have to double-check [his or her] work.

Who are your role models?
My father and siblings.

What would you tell a friend whose company was going through a slow time?
Keep marketing.

What would you tell someone whose business is growing faster than she can handle?
Do not be afraid to outsource or hire.

What's one mistake you won't make twice?
Assuming someone else cares as much as I do.

What was the best advice anybody ever gave you?
Trust and verify.

What couldn't you have done without?
A ton of time to work.

What do you like best about owning your own company?
The flexibility.

What do you like least?
I can't quit.

Describe your best day and your worst day.

The best day would be closing a deal. The worst day was [when we received] a letter from the IRS.

Does having your own business give you more or less freedom than working for someone else?

Much more. [If you] hire people [who are] better than you, then you have a lot of flexibility.

How has having your own business affected your marriage?

It has been work, but my husband runs a company as well.

What do your kids think about what you do?

They don't think about it.

Could you ever work for someone else again?

No.

What will you do next?

Retire.

How would a guy run your business differently?

Probably with less [of a] life balance. I could be much larger if I sold more, but the payoff for me is sending the kids off to school and then being there when they get home.

SARAH KUGELMAN is founder and president of skyn ICELAND, LLC, in New York City (*www.skyniceland.com*). Her company markets the only skincare line specifically formulated to counteract the detrimental effects of chronic stress on the skin. She is also the founder of gloss.com, a startup that she later sold to The Estée Lauder Companies.

How did you know it was time to start your own business?

I knew it was time to start my second when I couldn't get corporate management to buy into any of my ideas or proposals.

Did it feel like it was a big risk?
Yes, huge.

How much startup capital did it take?
$250,000.

Did you have a formal business plan laid out?
Yes.

How long was it until you were able to pay yourself?
It's been eighteen months and I'm still waiting.

Before you started your company, what were you totally clueless about?
Raising money and creating a corporate culture.

How do you find customers?
I make a consumer product so I sell to retailers who sell to end consumers. I find retailers through contacts, articles, trade publications, and referrals. I get customers directly via PR.

What's your finest wisdom on how to gain new business?
Have an active and extensive network. Don't be afraid to ask people for things. Always say thank you either with a gift or a card.

How did you know it was time to hire your first employee?
When I was sleeping three hours a night.

What's the secret to hiring the right people?
Listen to your gut. You know when you have the perfect person sitting in front of you.

How do you motivate or inspire your employees?
I really make them feel appreciated. I say thank you a lot. I get them involved in aspects of the business that go beyond their functional area so they feel a part of something bigger, so they don't just feel like a cog in the wheel but like an important member of a team that is building something incredible.

What's the most difficult thing about managing employees?
Dealing with all of the personalities. People come with emotions, problems, issues, and conflict. It takes a lot of patience and confidence to manage people.

How do you know when you have to fire someone?
You catch [the person] lying or demoralizing the rest of the team.

What do you tell yourself during slow times?
Tomorrow will be a better day. Running a business is always a roller coaster. Some days you think the earth is caving in, and the next day you are on top of the world. So when things are slow, you have to know it's a cycle.

What would you tell a friend whose company is going through a dry spell?
If she can afford it, take a vacation. Then, get new thinking and new blood into the company. Create an advisory board of experts. Bring on a team of MBAs to work on a strategic project. You'd be amazed at the big ideas people from diverse sources can bring to your business.

What would you tell someone whose business is growing faster than they can handle?
Focus on what is most important. You can't do everything. Even though everything seems equally important, it's not. Sit down and write three business objectives. If [something] on your list does not meet one of those objectives, throw it out.

What's the best advice anybody ever gave you?
Spend your time on the things that will make a difference in your business; e.g., instead of clearing out your e-mail's inbox, work on a project that will drive sales.

What's one mistake you won't make twice?
Going into business with my best friend.

Whom do you talk to when you need advice or a sounding board?
I have several mentors who have given me limitless support and advice. I also (for both of my companies) had an advisory board of high-level

executives and industry experts. I also get a lot of advice from my husband, [and my] mother and stepmother (both are high-level executives).

What couldn't you have done without?

My husband. His moral support was invaluable. He's also a banker and can help with the one aspect of the business I really don't like and don't feel completely comfortable with.

What do you like best about owning your own company?

Flexibility. It is a little bit of an illusion, since you think you will have more time to do the things you love but actually because you love what you're doing you end up having no time to do anything else.

What do you like least?

Payroll. It is nerve-wracking knowing you are responsible for people's sustenance. You're always worried you will hire people and not be able to pay them.

Describe your best day and your worst day.

My best day was announcing the sale of my first company, gloss.com, to The Estée Lauder Companies. My worst day was finding out my father had terminal lung cancer and not being able to take a plane to be with him because I had a board of directors who had just invested millions of dollars in me and were expecting major deliverables in a ridiculous time frame.

Does your business improve your lifestyle or make your life more difficult?

It improves my lifestyle because I love what I do and it constantly expands my world.

How has having your own business affected your marriage?

It has brought us together in some ways; taking a huge risk together and living through the development phase is a bond we'll share forever. But I don't have free evenings and weekends anymore. I force myself to take "husband time" to spend with him with no e-mails involved.

Could you ever work for someone else again?
No way!

What do you think you'll do next?
I said I'd retire after my first company, but that obviously didn't work. I would say, have a baby.

Do you have an exit plan?
I would like to sell my company or sell a majority interest to a strategic partner.

How would a guy run your business differently?
There would be a lot less drama!

☙ **MARILOU MCFARLANE** parlayed her many years in media sales with a San Francisco radio station into her own business, McFarlane Marketing, which provides media planning and execution for a variety of advertisers. She also is a partner in Blue Fire on Campus (*www.bluefireoncampus. com*), a brand promotion firm working exclusively with college campuses.

How did you know it was time to start your own business?
When the corporate culture changed dramatically where I worked and too many administrative, meaningless demands were made on my time, keeping me from focusing on what I was paid to do.

Did it feel like a big risk?
Yes.

How much startup capital did it take?
$5,000.

Did you have a formal business plan laid out?
No.

How long was it until you could pay yourself?
[Within the] first month.

Before you started your own company, what were you clueless about?
How tetherless and rudderless I would feel without bosses hovering in the wings!

How do you find clients?
Through existing relationships and research.

What's your finest wisdom on developing new business?
Treat each client or potential client with sincere care and respect for their time and their goals. Be persistent and don't take "no" personally.

What's the best advice anybody ever gave you?
It will take time, up to a year or more, but if you stay true to what you are trying to do, and work hard, you will begin to feel comfortable.

What's one mistake you won't make twice?
Rushing out of the gate without a detailed, formal business plan in place beforehand.

What couldn't you have done without?
My husband and a handful of great existing clients.

What do you like best about owning your own company?
The freedom and flexibility to create my own personal budgets and goals, without a gun to my head, and not having to generate meaningless reports or attend meaningless meetings.

What do you like least?
[I miss the] the camaraderie of being part of a larger team.

Does your business improve your lifestyle or make your life more difficult?
Improves it dramatically.

Does having your own business give you more or less freedom than working for someone else?
More.

How has having your own business affected your marriage?
It has strengthened it. Having support when you need it makes the relationship even stronger.

What do your kids think about what you do?
They are proud of me.

Could you ever work for someone else again?
Probably not.

How would a guy run your business differently?
He wouldn't be able to multitask to check off the to-do list every day, balancing the many business and child care/household things moms must do every day! ∎

Shared joy is a double joy; shared sorrow is half a sorrow.

Swedish proverb

ↇ

4

Grab Your Partner and Do-Si-Do

———

The decision whether or not to take a business partner is one of those questions with no wrong answer (and sometimes no right one either). A partner can make everything a lot more fun, and also means that you don't have to do it all yourself. On the other hand, the wrong partner can be disastrous.

One of the important things to consider when deciding whether or not to take a partner is that this is *not* a decision you have to live with for the rest of your life. All you have to decide is what will work best for you right now. You can change your mind later on. If you start out on your own and then decide you want to bring in a partner, you can certainly do that. Yes, it can be difficult and costly to dissolve a partnership, but it also can be done in a way that's mutually beneficial for all involved. And even if you have to break up with a partner and it gets ugly, it's not the end of the world. You'll get through it. As a friend of mine said: Put on your big-girl panties and deal with it!

Here's an example of how a partnership can change over time and evolve to suit each person's needs. I would never have had the guts to start my first agency without my partner, B.A. Together, we covered a wide spectrum of strengths and weaknesses, and were able to build a strong company quickly. Years later, after my son was born, B.A. and I began to differ in the amount of time and energy we wanted to give to work. So we dissolved our partnership through an agreement for her to buy out my half of the agency. MATCH is still thriving, and our friendship is too.

There are millions of reasons someone might make a good partner for you. Look for a person who has strengths where you have weaknesses. Choose someone you believe to be smarter than you in at least a few areas. Your personalities and styles may be nothing alike, but your missions for the company should be. Also keep in mind that a shared sense of humor can go a long way toward making the inevitable difficulties more bearable.

The cliché about a business partnership being like a marriage holds a lot of truth. It's a relationship that thrives on trust, on mutual values, on shared goals, and on a healthy dose of respect and affection for each other. Be sure to choose someone you'll enjoy spending a lot of time with—because you will be together more than you can imagine.

PT&Co.:
I'll Take a Baker's Dozen

Patrice Tanaka says that partners have always made her job easier. She has never felt lonely, the way she imagines some sole proprietors do, and has always taken comfort in being part of a group. Before Patrice launched PT&Co. she had spent eight years working with an incredibly difficult partner who, in many ways, was a good match for her. "We actually worked together really well," Patrice says. "She really loved to sell and hated to service, and I really loved to service and hated to sell. Our personalities were like polar opposites, but I never got in her way and she never got in mine."

Her first partner's demanding personality did take up a lot of emotional space, however. "Everything revolved around her," Patrice says. "She loved being front and center. I learned a lot from watching her—she was really brilliant and very creative and quick. But we could have been a lot more successful if it hadn't been all about her 24/7." Patrice also spent a lot of time and energy cleaning up after her partner's casual remarks, which frequently resulted in some messy relationship snags.

Even with its difficulties, Patrice feels that the partnership taught her many lessons about how she wanted to run her own business. "In hindsight, I see the value of that experience," she says. "I learned by witnessing somebody who did it in a way that was totally against what I believed—not just what I believe about managing people, but in terms of living by the golden rule."

Patrice's mother always stressed the importance of sharing. Maybe that's why, when she launched PT&Co., Patrice felt compelled to share the company with not just one partner, but twelve. "I probably wouldn't do it again," she admits. "But at the time, it seemed like the natural thing to do. We had thirteen co-owners who founded the company. I felt like if thirteen of us were going to take a chance, everybody should be an owner. Everybody should have a piece of the action."

Patrice's lawyer and accountant both thought she was insane for wanting to have thirteen co-owners. The lawyer negotiating the deal actually begged her not to do it. "He said to me, 'It's difficult enough for any new business to succeed, even with just one owner,'" she recalls. "He kept telling me, 'The problems are magnified if you have two owners, but thirteen owners? That is just not going to work.'"

Patrice eventually overrode that legal opinion. "I finally said, I really value your opinion and I love you dearly, but there is no more discussion. This is the way it's going to be. So your job is to fix an agreement so that we can have [thirteen partners]."

The team used a no-pain-no-gain approach to assign percentage of ownership. Each partner's percentage of shares corresponded to the pay decrease she agreed to take to get the company off the ground. Because Patrice was taking the biggest salary cut, she ended up with the largest stake in the business.

Though the deal was made with the best intentions, complications arose later for the thirteen partners. Patrice says, "What I didn't realize at the time was that everybody was at a different stage in their lives. We were spread across the age spectrum from mid-twenties to mid-forties. Maturity levels were very different." Some of the partners' attitudes tended toward "I'm an owner; I can do whatever I want." Others embraced the philosophy of working even harder as an owner and putting the good of the group before their own needs.

That range of perspectives made even the simplest decisions complicated. "It's not as if everybody felt the same way on any given subject," Patrice remembers. "Can you imagine thirteen people trying to come to an agreement on a shareholders' agreement? It took years. So a lot of time and energy was spent trying to get the group to come to a common agreement about what ownership meant and what our responsibilities and expectations of each other were." This process diverted attention from what the group most needed to be doing—growing the business, building a brand, and serving clients.

Patrice's agency is currently run by four of the original thirteen partners. "It's amazing because it's only the four of us and so we can actually come to an agreement really quickly. We are all on the same page," says Patrice. In contrast to the complex and drawn-out negotiations of the first ownership agreement with the thirteen-person team, the foursome was able to reach a shareholders' agreement within just six weeks.

"We're very different in personalities, the four of us," Patrice says of her current situation. She adds, "The thing we share in common is that all four women work really hard and always go ten steps beyond, and are willing to put their money on the line."

Although they are collaborative in spirit, the four current partners have four clearly defined territories. Patrice is CEO and creative director; two other partners each hold the title of president and act as director for a specific list of client categories. The fourth partner is the CFO, so she handles the money.

On the PT&Co. Web site, there is one link marked "Co-founders/ owners." If you click on it, you will see a few photos of the four women together in front of the photographer's backdrop. They're all dressed in sophisticated black for their corporate headshots, but they're crowded together in a tight foursome—all seemingly talking at once and completely cracking themselves up. It does indeed look like more fun than trying to do it on your own.

KooKoo Bear Kids:
It's All in the Family

Tara Mediate started her company with a built-in partner: her husband, Joe. Since this was a second startup for the two of them, they already knew they made good business partners. The new factor in the equation for this particular company was bringing in Tara's sister, Trace.

In the early days, Trace had acted as a behind-the-scenes advisor and pitched in nights and weekends on everything from producing the first catalog to packing and shipping merchandise. As the company began to pick up steam, Tara realized she needed someone who could take over the Herculean task of getting subsequent catalogs produced. If Trace wasn't going to come on board, they needed to find someone else who would.

Tara took her sister to lunch to talk about it at length. She understood she was asking a lot of Trace, who had a good salary and career stability where she was working. Tara says she told her sister, "We could go under. I can't guarantee you it's going to make it, but you can always find another job. If you want to do it, it's a risk you're going to have to take." Tara also says that she knew Trace would like being on her own and not having anybody telling her what hours she had to work, and that it would be a different type of work—a fun challenge. Not long after the lunch, Trace came on board full-time, and became the only one of the three partners to draw a salary.

Although Joe and Tara still own and control the company, they've given Trace a percentage that they hope will pay off for her in the future. "It will build and build for her," says Tara. "Her part will be more and more as the years go by."

In the day-to-day operation of the company, Tara, Trace, and Joe have distinct areas of responsibility and they don't seem to cross over into each other's territory at all. "We have very definite roles. We have our strengths and no one steps over their boundaries," Tara says. Tara buys the products and oversees customer service. Joe handles the financial end of things and deals with marketing tasks such as buying the mailing lists. Trace handles the production of the catalog.

Tara feels that boundaries are of primary importance in sustaining harmonious partnerships—especially for partnerships that include the bonds of sisterhood and marriage. She says, "There's a fine line there and none of us ever jumps over it."

That doesn't mean the group is immune to tension between the objectives of their individual areas within the company. Tara often finds herself caught between her other two partners. "It gets difficult because

Joe has a financial mind and Trace has a creative mind," Tara says. "It is a difficult situation because I'm in the middle. You don't want to take sides—that will never work. You try to see each situation. I'm the peace-maker."

Ultimately, they all have to be cognizant of how their individual areas affect the company as a whole. "We talk about things," Tara says. "All of us are big enough to admit it when we screw up."

Tara thinks one of the reasons she and Joe work so well together is that they had to work out the kinks of constant togetherness when he sold his first company and was suddenly hanging around the house all day. "When Joe sold his business and stopped traveling, that was very tough for us," she says. "I was used to him leaving and traveling, and being by myself with the kids."

Tara was so accustomed to handling the kids alone while Joe was on the road that it took her a while to realize that she needed to keep him in the loop. "Communication was huge," she says. "At first, I just kept right on doing my own thing. I would never tell him anything. He was like, Where are you? Where do you go? When are you guys coming home? I was picking the kids up, going wherever. I don't think he realized before what it's like to be a mom."

Now they share the carpooling duties, but communication is key there as well. Sometimes they're both involved at the office and neither wants to break away from what they're doing. "That's a tug of war," Tara says. "Who's busier and who really needs to be here?"

For Tara and Joe, there is also a point at which too much com-munication can be detrimental to their relationship. "I don't want to talk about business at night or on weekends or when we all go away somewhere," says Tara. "In the beginning, with a startup, you have no choice. But there's always a constant need to regroup when you have your own business. You have to get back to reality and remind yourself what's important. My family's important; my kids are important." They have set boundaries on when they will and won't talk business to prevent it from seeping into the time they have together as a couple or a family. But it is the overlap of business and family that make Tara and Joe work together so well as partners. As she puts it, "We're not just sharing the business; we're sharing the kids as well."

Financial Stress Reduction:
Thanks, but No Thanks

From time to time, various people have suggested that they would like to be Chellie's business partner, but she has always resisted the idea strongly. She says she doesn't even want to be big enough for an employee, much less a full-fledged partner—partly because of what she sees as the dismal success rate for business partnerships.

"Partnerships are very difficult," she says. "I have a friend who is an attorney and he drafts a lot of partnership agreements. And then he drafts a lot of partnership dissolutions. It's like the marriage rate. How many result in divorce?" Chellie's point is not one to ignore. Various sources claim that a stunning 50 to 70 percent of all business partnerships fail, although what looks like failure to some may just be moving on for others.

"I think it's probably hard to find the correct balance with a partner. It's so easy for people to start feeling out of balance about it. One of you feels like you're contributing more and the other one's not working enough. Somebody goes on vacation and there's a problem. It's difficult."

Chellie also feels her independent streak might make a partnership more difficult for her than it is for others. "One of the guiding principles of my life is that I don't like to be told what to do," she says. "That's probably why I'm not married. I don't like criticism; I don't welcome it. I don't want anybody telling me what's wrong with me or the way I'm

instant wisdom

ON PARTNERSHIPS

Whether you decide to take a partner or not, you can always change your mind later.

What works for you now might not work down the road—you can try something else.

If you do choose to start a business with a partner, look for someone who brings strengths to the table that are different from the ones you have.

Make sure your values, goals, and expectations are in general alignment with those of your partner.

Pick someone you will enjoy hanging out with, because you'll probably be together for more time than you expect.

The more partners you have, the exponentially more complicated it gets.

The partnership relationship is like a marriage, in that it takes work. Don't worry; it's worth it.

doing things. So I stay away from any structure that's going to put me in a position to hear something like that."

Another of Chellie's guiding principles is to keep life as easy as possible. For her, it would be much more difficult to deal with having a business partner than to operate on her own. It's not too difficult to see why she prefers to take a pass on this one. ∎

🎋 **B. A. ALBERT** is the owner and CEO of MATCH, Inc. (*www.matchinc. com*), a full-service advertising agency. Her company was named one of the ten fastest-growing women-owned firms in Atlanta.

Did it feel like a big risk to start your company?
It was a bigger risk not to.

How much startup capital did it take?
$10,000 each for the two of us.

Did you have a formal business plan laid out?
Just a list of steps we had to take scribbled on index cards.

How long was it until you were able to pay yourself?
About two months, which was a month or two earlier than we'd expected.

Before you started your agency, what were you clueless about?
Everything.

What's the secret to hiring the right people?
Always hire people who are smarter than you.

How do you motivate your employees?
Laugh. Tell the truth. Be your best.

What's the most difficult thing about managing employees?
Loving them all equally.

How do you know when it's time to fire someone?
When you can't look the person in the eye.

What do you tell yourself during slow times?
Time to go fishing.

What would you tell a friend whose company is going through a dry spell?
Throw a party. When you open your door, good things come in.

What's the best advice anybody ever gave you?
You're only as good as the last ad you did.

What's one mistake you won't make twice?
Hiring a client's kid.

What couldn't you have done without?
My business partner, Elizabeth.

What do you like best about owning your own company?
Everything.

What do you like least?
If I'm not having fun, it's my own damn fault.

Describe your best day and your worst day.
Hiring. And firing.

What do your parents think about what you do?
They don't understand why I can't put my name on the ads.

What do you think you'll do next?
I'd like to be a dock master on a remote part of the Florida coast.

Do you have an exit plan?
I plan to exit while I am still young enough to play.

How would a guy run your business differently?
Less food, less tears, less laughter.

꙳ **SUSAN MESSLER** is president of Traffic Management Services, Inc., (*www.e-tms.net*), a third-party logistics and transportation management firm in Charlotte, North Carolina.

Did it feel like a big risk to start your own business?
Yes.

Before you started your company, what were you clueless about?
Running a business.

Did you have a formal business plan laid out?
Yes.

How did you find clients?
References and word of mouth.

What's your finest wisdom on how to develop new business?
Honesty, quality, and references from other customers.

How do you motivate or inspire your employees?
Team effort and flexibility.

What's the most difficult thing about managing employees?
Individual personalities.

How do you know when it's time to fire someone?
They're not part of the team.

What do you tell yourself during slow times?
It will turn around.

What would you tell a friend whose company is going through a dry spell?
Hang in there.

What would you tell someone whose business is growing faster than she can handle?
Hire as many people as you can.

What's the best advice anybody ever gave you?
Be honest and as close to perfect as you can.

What's one mistake you won't make twice?
Handing off responsibility to employees before they're ready.

What do you like best about owning your own company?
Making everything work, and the flexibility.

What do you like least?
Stress and hours.

Could you ever work for someone else again?
Probably not.

How has having your own business affected your marriage?
My husband and I own the business together.

How would a guy run your business differently?
Probably not as organized or detailed.

NANCY C. JUNEAU is the CEO of Juneau Construction Company (*www. juneaucc.com*) in Atlanta. Her company is a commercial general contracting and construction management company. It's also one of the largest female-owned companies in Georgia.

How did you know it was time to start your own business?
There never is a good time. I had just had my third child!

Did it feel like a big risk?
Yes.

How much startup capital did it take?
$50,000.

How long was it before you were able to pay yourselves?
We were able to from the beginning, because we factored six months' living expenses into the startup costs.

What's the trick to successful cash flow?
Timely billing.

How do you motivate or inspire your employees?
By making them feel appreciated, thanking them, and rewarding them.

What do you tell yourself during slow times?
We will get through this.

Whom do you talk to when you need a sounding board?
My husband.

What do you like best about owning your own company?
The sense of ownership.

What do you like least?
Responsibility for employees.

Does your business improve your lifestyle or make it more difficult?
It improves it very much.

Does having your own business give you more or less freedom than working for someone else?
More.

What do your kids think about what you do?
They love it. They're very proud.

Could you ever work for someone else again?
No.

What do you think you'll do next?
Be more involved in my community.

How would a guy run your business differently?
My husband and I started the company together. I am better suited as CEO and he is a better president. We definitely complement each other in that our strengths and weaknesses balance us out. ■

There are two ways of being creative. One can sing and dance.
Or one can create an environment
in which singers and dancers can flourish.

Warren Bennis

∽

5

Where You Go When You Go to Work

———

Many things have shifted in the business climate of the past several years and one of those is the level of respect now accorded to the home office. It used to be that a home office was considered not quite legitimate—as if anyone working from home wasn't really serious about it. A home office worker was often thought to be one of those mothers who just dabbled in a career, half-trying to make a go of it. Now the home office is one of the fastest growing places to do business in America.

Why is the home office suddenly legit? For one thing, Daniel Pink made being a free agent cool with his 2002 book titled *Free Agent Nation: The Future of Working for Yourself.* Technology made a few more leaps and bounds toward leveling the playing field between large companies with deep pockets and lone entrepreneurs with just enough money for a decent computer system. The robust growth in the information economy meant fewer Americans were turning to manufacturing and industrial jobs, and more were building careers in knowledge-based industries, from technology to advertising to law. Although it wouldn't be practical to set up a factory at home, it's quite simple to crank up a computer in the spare bedroom when what you sell is largely in your head. The dot-com crash, along with the wave of downsizing that swept through almost all industries in the last handful of years, meant that a lot of men were suddenly in business for themselves. The fact that more men were doing it went a long way toward taking the notion of home business into the arena of real business.

More and more smart people now run their own businesses from home, using the same brains they formerly used on the staff of large companies. As they say in advertising, the inventory goes down the elevator every night. It's not the marble lobbies and corporate art collections that make things happen. It's brains and experience and talent. And you can take all of that home with you and set up shop right there.

Many entrepreneurs rave about the comforts of a home office. First on the list for many is the elimination of any commute, which adds precious time to your life. If your client contact is largely by phone and e-mail, you get to skip the suits and pantyhose most days. Some mothers love being home-based because they can be easily accessible to their children—others find that it makes them way too accessible. A few potential downsides include the isolation you may feel without the camaraderie of jovial coworkers, and the potential awkwardness of hosting client meetings in an office that looks more like a spare bedroom than a professional place of business.

An actual office out in the real world has its own advantages and disadvantages. If your clients will be coming to you, then you will almost certainly want to have traditional office space. Or you might consider leasing an office address you use only for client meetings. In many cities, companies like Intelligent Office (*www.intelligentoffice.com*) lease executive suites and the occasional use of conference rooms on an as-needed basis. Your office is a huge part of your brand. Clients and potential clients will walk through the door and immediately judge your company's success, values, personality, and style based on the first glimpse of your space. (They're not being shallow—it's just human nature to make snap judgments.) Consider the distinctly different impressions you would make advising a client from behind a standard-issue wood laminate workstation, an antique French farm table, or an ultrahip, stainless steel desk.

Many people who make the move from a home office to regular office space discover an unexpected benefit to physically leaving their office at the end of the day. Somehow, that makes it easier to leave work behind mentally as well.

Perhaps the biggest disadvantage to leasing office space for a startup is the extra expense. But sometimes there's a way around that. When B.A. and I were about to start MATCH, we went to see some space a friend was subleasing in an old turn-of-the-century factory. We unlocked the door to reveal twenty-foot-high brick walls and wide-planked hardwood floors scarred by honest work. It was the perfect place to start an ad agency. We had no budget for office space, but came up with a plan for a highly creative one-year lease agreement. We paid zero rent for the first three months, then regular rent for the next six, and then double rent for the final three months. At the end of the year, we took over the lease from our friend and also leased some adjoining space.

PT&Co.:
An Office with All the Extras

Patrice feels strongly that the office environment affects the caliber of work that people are able to do. The way she sees it, the workplace contains the business's soul, and nurturing that soul should be a key goal for those running a company. When she had first negotiated the buyback deal with Chiat/Day, her basic concern was simply having a place—any place—to hang her hat.

Part of disentangling from Chiat/Day was getting out of a high-priced lease that was not practical in a financial downturn. But Patrice and her team had no idea where they would find affordable space, especially since they had no history as a company, no banking relationship, and almost none of the basic information they'd need to fill in the blanks on a standard office lease application.

Then Patrice ran into the owner of another public relations agency. His company had also been hit hard by the failing economy, and he had decided to fold his Manhattan office. His space was already set up for a PR group that was coincidentally the same size as Patrice's new agency. She told him her story, and he decided to help her out because, he said, somebody had helped him when he was starting his own business. He even let Patrice keep all the furniture and equipment so her company was able to come in and be up and running immediately. "We moved with nothing but our computers and all our files stuffed in shopping bags," Patrice remembers.

PT&Co. has since moved to another building, this time in the West Village near the Meatpacking District. At the center of the office is a living room where employees often gather to relax on the couch. Patrice says the living room is as much a statement as a place to hang out. She doesn't want an office where workers are confined to a claustrophobic cubicle. There's a kitchen, lunchroom, and even a meditation space. "Since so much of our life is spent in the office," she reasons, "the office should surely include some living space." The meditation room, dedicated solely to providing employees with a quiet retreat, is a peaceful oasis of white walls and gray carpet, with diffused sunlight pouring in through the opaque window blinds. "We're hit with so many messages during a day," says Patrice. "The soul needs some quiet to recover from that. Meditation helps us center. It makes you more energized." The meditation room is also used for the occasional nap—which is fine with Patrice. "Sometimes you're tired," she says. "You need a nap. I don't want the office to be a place of relentless work. You have to take care of the needs of the body."

She also believes in the need for fun. Various employees take on the role of cruise director, planning staff parties and outings. Every Thursday in the summer, for instance, they announce at 4:00 P.M. that margaritas will now be served on the Fiesta Deck, which turns out to be the office kitchen.

The office does contain some cubicles, but the cozy red and intense purple walls add visual relief, along with the bright, airy spaces and varied textures—not to mention the original art and fresh flowers.

The benefits of creating this sort of nurturing workspace go beyond pampered employees, to Patrice's mind. "We work hard. Everybody here works extremely hard. We need to be operating at optimal power and speed to keep up with what we need to do for our clients."

Creating a sense of community in the workplace is also a priority for Patrice. "So many people who live in New York have come here from other places. For a lot of people, the workplace community is all they have."

Once again, Patrice cites her upbringing in the communal island atmosphere of Hawaii as inspiration for her community motivations at work. "We're here together and we're necessary to each other," she says, "and I want us to be helpful to one another so that we can make things work for us and for our clients."

KooKoo Bear Kids:
The Business That Swallowed a Suburban Home

Having already successfully started a software company in an apartment, it seemed reasonable to Tara and Joe to launch a catalog from the house. In many ways it was easier for Tara to keep her business and family lives part of one seamless entity. Although she worked some long hours, the kids could glance up from their video games or breeze in from the backyard whenever they felt the need for her attention. She could shuttle the kids back and forth to school and other activities, help with homework in the afternoons, and go back to work in her office off the family room after they'd been tucked into bed at night.

But the home office situation grew increasingly chaotic as business picked up. The samples and inventory filled the basement and began creeping upstairs. The family squeezed into one or two rooms while all the other rooms in the house were styled and lit for various catalog photo shoots. Tara and Joe finally decided that their sanity was worth the cost of office space.

"I wanted to be no more than three miles from my kids' school and I wanted to be no more than three miles from my house," Tara says. They found a small storefront; it was expensive, but the location was right. "It's perfect," Tara says. "I can be anywhere, the school or home, in eight minutes." Six months later they rented the larger space behind their office to serve as a warehouse, but they waited until they couldn't stand it one more second before taking on that extra rent. "It was getting overwhelming because there was so much going on in such a little space," Tara says. "But expanding into the other space was a big step for us because you're adding on so much more a month financially. We rode it out until we were very, very close to the breaking point and at our wit's end. My advice to someone else would be to wait until it's really, really painful." Tara and Joe recently took on one more lease for a storefront across the street where they are opening a retail shop and outlet.

The office décor at KooKoo Bear Kids is startup basic, studded with cute painted wooden signs and other colorful samples from the catalog. Trace's office is neat and functional, while Tara's is filled with towering stacks of merchandise. People wear whatever they want, leaning toward the extreme end of business casual, since their only contact with customers is by phone.

Sometimes one or more of Tara and Joe's brood will be hanging around. The customer service reps occasionally bring their children in if a babysitter calls in sick or one of the kids isn't feeling well. To Tara, it seems that a child in the office is no more out of place than a stack of office work at the kitchen table. Being a mom isn't something she keeps separate from her business, and her business isn't something she considers separate from her kids.

Financial Stress Reduction:
Moving Home to the Den

Many entrepreneurs (such as Tara) start their businesses at home and eventually work their way up to needing real office space. Chellie Campbell did the opposite. She started her Financial Stress Reduction workshops in the conference room of her bookkeeping business office, and then opted for the joys of working from home.

When she started, she would go in every day to work in the office, teaching the workshops in the conference room in the evenings. Chellie's housemate called her attention to the absurdity of that setup. She asked Chellie why she would drive to work every day and pay rent for office space when she could teach the classes at home. Chellie and her roommate surmised that the den would be a perfect setting. Chellie remembers asking her roommate, "You wouldn't mind? Doing the workshops here would mean there would be a lot of people coming in and out of the house."

Her roommate shrugged and said, "I like people." So Chellie moved the business home, taking over one spare bedroom as her office and the den for workshops.

The only remaining hurdle for Chellie was affording the move from the office to home. "I was going to have to hire movers and I needed an organizer to help me organize the move, and I needed to pay money to totally redo all my business stationery and business cards." She combed through her networking contacts. Chellie discovered a printer, an organizer, and a mover who all wanted to take her workshop. They agreed to provide their services for free and she let them take the class at no charge. The move cost her nothing.

From there, all Chellie had to do was arrange the furniture. The den already had a game table for poker nights, and a couch and loveseat, so all Chellie added was a handful of folding chairs.

One of the last remaining issues for Chellie to do business at home was a city business license. Chellie registered herself as a sole practitioner, after briefly considering incorporating. "Some people say if you incorporate, you would save some money in taxes. But there aren't a whole lot of things you can deduct in a corporation that you can't deduct as business expenses in a sole proprietorship. With a corporation, you have to file [many] forms every year, and do payroll and payroll taxes, and I just can't be bothered. One of my rules is 'Keep it simple.'"

When a neighbor expressed concern over the number of cars that were parking on their residential street, Chellie reminded the woman nicely that the class was only four hours a week, on Monday and Wednesday nights. "That was the end of any problem with parking," she says.

Chellie sees huge benefits in having people come to her for the workshops. "Do you know how much of my life I get back from not doing two-hour commutes every day?" she asks rhetorically. "I spend no time commuting."

However, working from home does not mean working in a bathrobe for Chellie. "People have this illusion that you work from home in your pajamas, sitting up in bed," she says. "But if I'm in my bed, I'm sleeping. I can't work like that." From the years she spent in acting, Chellie has learned that costume is important to her. She makes her sales phone calls in business attire and makeup because, she says, it helps her speak more

instant wisdom
ON WHERE TO PUT YOUR OFFICE

If you can't afford to pay for the space you want, try to figure out another way to get it. You'd be surprised how many people like to lend a helping hand to startups.

Where you do business can have a huge effect on how you do business. Choose a place that makes you feel inspired and comfortable.

Think: location, location, location. One of the best perks of owning your own business is being able to work somewhere that requires little to no commute. If you're combining work and kids, this is even more important.

Create an office that includes everything you need to work at your best. Consider elements like fresh flowers, sunlight, good music, windows that open, and a place to exercise—and maybe even a meditation room.

professionally. Of course, business attire for Chellie means metallic-gold sneakers, so it's not like she's spending all day in pantyhose.

When Chellie initially decided to move her business home, she worried that she might feel too isolated or trapped in one place. She reasoned that if she didn't like it, she could always rent another office somewhere. Instead, the move has transformed her life.

"As soon as I moved my classroom into the den area of the house, my life became really simple and really rich. I live my life my way. I love my life." It's hard to argue with that. ■

▶ **DEBBIE SCOPPECHIO** is CEO of Creative Alliance (*www.cre8.com*), an integrated advertising, marketing, and promotions firm in Louisville, Kentucky.

Before you started your company, what were you totally clueless about?
The bottom line.

How did you know it was time to start your own company?
I realized I was a leader in building two other advertising agencies for someone else.

Did it feel like a big risk?
No.

Did you have a formal business plan?
Yes.

How much capital did it take?
None. Just furniture donated by clients.

When were you able to pay yourself?
Very quickly, but very little.

You couldn't have done it without what?
My creative partners and my accountant.

What do you like best about owning your own company?
Everything.

What do you like the least?
Nothing.

How has having your own business affected your marriage?
I'm divorced and remarried to an understanding, strong man.

Who are your role models?
David Novak, CEO of Yum Brands, my mother, and my first boss in my advertising career.

Does your business improve your lifestyle or make it more difficult?
I love what I do and I love my clients, so I would say it improves my lifestyle.

What's the best advice anyone ever gave you?
Be yourself and be confident.

How did you know it was time to hire your first employee?
The workload was 24/7 plus. I needed a team to work with and feed off.

What's the secret to good hiring?
Attitude and culture check.

When do you have to fire someone?
When either their attitude or work hurts the rest of the team.

What's the most difficult thing about managing employees?
Keeping them positive, and inspiring and motivating them.

What the secret to successful cash flow?
A good CFO.

What's your best advice on how to win new business?
Understand what the client needs. Do your homework. Be persistent. Offer value.

How do you find new clients?
Networking, building a reputation, phone calls, mailings, never giving up.

What would you tell someone whose business is growing faster than they can handle?
Be careful and handle it! Grow smart. Hire smart. Make sure you always deliver, if not overdeliver.

What would you tell a friend going through a dry spell?
Don't give up. Brainstorm ideas to grow your team and get them charged up.

Could you ever work for someone else again?
I doubt it, but never say never.

How would a guy run your business differently?
He wouldn't have my energy and determination. He wouldn't have my patience. He wouldn't have the team loyalty. In short, I don't think he would be as successful.

What do you think you'll do next?
Train entry-level account service people

❧ **PATRICIA C. SIBLEY** is president and owner of Media Solutions (*www. mediasolutions-atl.com*), a media-buying company in Atlanta. Her company makes recommendations to clients on how to best spend advertising dollars, and then implements those plans.

How did you know it was time to start your own business?
I just knew the timing was right.

Did it feel like a big risk?
No.

How much startup capital did it take?
Not much because I started it out of my house and kept my overhead low.

Did you have a formal business plan laid out?
No. I grew out of what I wanted to do with my business.

How long was it before you could pay yourself?
Three to four months.

Before you started your company, what were you clueless about?
Running a company.

How do you find clients?
Word of mouth.

What's the secret to a successful cash flow?
Keeping your overhead low so there's money left over that you can save for a rainy day.

How did you know it was time to hire your first employee?
When I was working eighteen-hour days and still missing deadlines.

What's the secret to hiring the right people?
Listening to their answers and watching their faces when you interview them.

How do you motivate or inspire your employees?
I treat them with respect and let them know that I am here for them.

What's the most difficult thing about managing employees?
Finding time to be a good manager; show you care—but not get too involved in their personal lives.

How do you know when it's time to fire someone?
They're late.

What do you tell yourself during slow times?
You've been through them before. It only takes one phone call to change your slow times into fast ones.

What would you tell a friend whose business was going through a dry spell?
It happens. If you have a good company/product—you'll be fine.

What's the best advice anybody ever gave you?
Keep your overhead low, pay cash for everything, don't take on debt.

What's one mistake you won't make twice?
Having a partner.

What couldn't you have done without?
My CPA, lawyer, banker, business friends who started their own business.

What do you like best about owning your own company?
Being able to choose whom I want to work with.

What do you like least?
Paperwork related to owning your company.

Does having your own business give you more or less freedom than working for someone else?
More freedom.

How has having your own business affected your marriage?
My husband knew about my business and the way I work before we got married so there's never been a problem. He is very understanding.

Could you ever work for someone else again?
No.

What do you think you'll do next?
Own another business (maybe in another field).

How would a guy run your business differently?
I don't think he would change very much. Might take a few more risks than I do.

ROBIN KOCINA is owner, operator, and president of Mid-America Events & Expos, Inc., a thriving event-management and exposition company based in Minneapolis, Minnesota. She is also co-owner and CFO of Media Relations, Inc., a pay-per-interview public relations and marketing company, and co-owner of Kocina Marketing Companies, Inc.

What's your finest wisdom on how to gain new business?
Underpromise and overdeliver.

How did you find customers?
The best way is to give great customer service and ask for referrals.

What's the secret to a successful cash flow?
Don't overextend yourself.

What's the secret to hiring the right people?
A comprehensive hiring plan.

How do you know when it's time to fire someone?
They don't show up for work.

What do you like best about owning your own company?
The people I work with. Watching them grow.

What do you like least?
Can't think of anything.

What would you tell someone whose business is growing faster than she can handle?
Ask for help; use outside contractors.

What would you tell a friend whose company is going through a dry spell?
Work harder. The rewards will come.

Could you ever work for someone else again?
No.

What do you think you'll do next?
Charity work.

Did it feel like a big risk to you to start your own business?
Yes.

How much startup capital did it take?
$10,000 to start our first company.

How long was it until you could pay yourself?
Years, but it now pays very well.

Did you have a formal business plan laid out?
Yes, but not real formal.

How do you motivate or inspire your employees?
Let them be a part of the company growth.

What's the most difficult thing about managing employees?
All the different personalities.

What do you tell yourself during slow times?
This is only temporary.

Whom do you talk to when you need advice or a sounding board?
Other business owners.

Does your business improve your lifestyle or make your life more difficult?
It improves my lifestyle.

Does having your own business give you more or less freedom than working for someone else?
More freedom.

How has having your own business affected your marriage?
It has been both a positive and a negative to our marriage, but after seventeen years we've learned to focus on the positive.

What do your kids think about what you do?
I think they are proud.

Do you have an exit plan?
I'm working on an exit plan.

How would a guy run your business differently?

[He] would take a less personal approach. I care about each of my employees and try to determine where their strengths are so I can match them to the job.

DONNA ROSEN is the owner of Donna Rosen, Artists' Representative in Brookville, Maryland. She represents freelance illustrators and works with art directors to help them get the illustrations they want.

How did you know it was time to start your own business?

I hated the rat race. I fell into this when an illustrator friend asked me to represent him. I figured I would give it a try, and it snowballed into a full-time career.

Did it feel like a big risk to you to start your own business?

It felt like a risk, but the other options felt even riskier.

How much startup capital did it take to start your company?

None. We have no overhead or product. I bought a computer and sort of bartered services for advertising until we got to the point where we could afford the tools of the trade.

Did you have a formal business plan laid out?

No. I don't know that I'd recommend winging it like I did, but this was more of a part-time endeavor that evolved into a full-time business.

How long was it before you could afford to pay yourself?

It took a while for the jobs to be steady enough to amount to anything. I was only doing it part-time at first since it wasn't providing enough money to live. When jobs started to come in a bit more frequently, I decided to dedicate myself to it full-time, and it started to become more financially supportive.

Before you started your company, what were you clueless about?

How much self-discipline it would take to work from home.

How do you find your clients?

I rely on advertising in illustration directories, direct mailings of sample work, networking, periodic mass e-mails, and good old-fashioned leg-work—showing portfolios at every possible opportunity.

How do you motivate or inspire your illustrators?

Most of them are self-motivated. They enjoy what they do and what they create and I like to reinforce their efforts and talents with praise and, of course, more assignments.

What's the most difficult thing about managing people?

In my business, it is keeping egos in check.

Do you ever have to end a relationship with an illustrator you've taken on?

Sometimes. I know it's time to sever the relationship when they don't take assignments seriously and begin to miss deadlines or turn in halfhearted, shoddy work.

What's your finest wisdom on developing new business?

Be likeable.

What couldn't you have done without?

The huge talent of the artists I work with.

What do you like best about owning your own company?

Being my own boss with no one telling me what to do or when to do it. Sometimes a tough day is deciding between a mid-afternoon nap or a bath—it is rare to be able to do both.

What do you like least?

Having the phone as my new umbilical cord. I am holding off on a Blackberry but I know that day is coming.

What do you read for business inspiration?

I just look at the pretty pictures.

What do you tell yourself during slow times?

This, too, shall pass. There are seasonal lulls and I have to keep reminding myself that this is an annual thing and not to stress. Then I go to a matinee.

What would you tell a friend whose company is going through a dry spell?

It would depend. Many businesses go through slow periods, but if it is a trend that is likely to continue, then she should figure out a way to keep up with the current trends and directions of their market.

What would you tell someone whose business is growing faster than she can handle?

Don't let it get to the point where you can't control it, because efficiency and productivity go down. It's better to do less but do well than to spread yourself too thin and do poorly.

What's the best advice anybody ever gave you?

Never ask anyone to do anything that you wouldn't do yourself.

What's one mistake you won't make twice?

Going against my gut when it comes to taking on a new illustrator who is difficult, regardless of talent.

Describe your best day and your worst day.

On the best days the phone rings with many exciting jobs. Artists turn in their assignments and we get lots of rave reviews. On the worst there are communication problems and an unhappy art director.

Does your business improve your lifestyle or make your life more difficult?

It makes my life much easier and less stressful. Working from home allows me to avoid a long commute. I don't need to dress for work. I can take my tools of the trade with me, so I am able to get out of the office for trips to the gym or lunch with a friend or I can slip out early to attend lectures or events downtown. Every day is different, so I don't get bored.

Does having your own business give you more or less freedom than working for someone else?
Absolutely more. I don't punch a clock. I can work early in the morning or late at night. (Or both, if I choose to.) I have even negotiated jobs while sitting on the beach in Mexico.

How has having your own business affected your relationships?
It has made me much better able to deal with not being married. I am proud to be able to fend for myself. I like the satisfaction of knowing that anything I have comes from my own hard work.

Could you ever work for someone else again?
Possibly with someone as a partner, but never for someone. No way.

What do you think you'll do next?
I'd like to continue doing this, as long as there is a need for it. I enjoy working with creative people. As the field evolves or changes I hope to keep up, possibly branching into other areas of the same field.

Do you have an exit plan?
No, but at this point I don't plan an exit.

How would a guy run your business differently?
I think that women are typically more empathetic and better listeners, so I have more of a personal relationship with many of the artists I represent than a man would. These characteristics make me better able to deal with issues that concern ego or emotion. That's often required in problem-solving situations. ■

Nature does not hurry, yet everything is accomplished.

LaoTzu

Ɛ⁏Ɔ

6

How Was Your Day?

———

Some of us put off doing what we really want to be doing because we think we'll get to it later. Any major goal in life is achieved not in one fell swoop but by many small actions that pile up, day after day, and year after year. Our quality of life is established in the here and now, not in some future dream life that we'll get around to after we get all this other stuff done. If we spend our days stressed out, frustrated, and resentful, then eventually that's what our whole life becomes. If we instead create for ourselves days that are fun and satisfying, productive and meaningful, then they add up to a life that is all those things as well.

Imagine the kind of life you'd like to lead and then reflect that in your daily calendar. If one of your big things is staying fit, start using lunch time to go to the gym. If you want more time with your kids, end your workday at 3:00 P.M. Like to sleep in? Do it. One of the benefits of owning your own business is that you can decide to do any or all of the above. My dream life includes writing fiction, so I generally spend one morning of my Tribe workweek struggling earnestly with my novel. I also want my life to include plenty of time with my son. So when my work is interrupted by a little boy catapulting through the dog door and onto my office floor, I try to take a short break to play around with him. We all have twenty-four hours in a day. Owning your own business gives you more control over how you use those hours, and thus how you spend your life.

Many, if not all, of the women interviewed for this book have mentioned the appeal of time sovereignty, although perhaps not in those exact words. Most of us don't care so much if we have to work hard. What's important to us is that we have the ability to choose *when*. Almost any woman business owner you ask will say that she has more to do in a day than she can realistically get done. Especially if she has kids, she's bound to be stretched thin. But what you'll also hear, in most cases, is that there's nothing she's doing that she'd want to give up. More than any other group of people, women who own their own businesses tend to feel that they're living their own life exactly the way they want to live it. Day in and day out.

PT&Co.:
Dancing the Day Away

Patrice says that for years she prayed to find something in her life she enjoyed as much as her work. She finds her creative challenges, personal meaning, and feeling of community within her agency. At times, she even finds her professional hurdles to be something of a spiritual journey. For years, she had only an occasional urge to look outside of work for her life fulfillment.

"When you love your work, that's all you want to do," she says. "But sometimes, I used to find myself thinking, okay, I've worked yet another twelve-hour day. I've got to work this weekend. I'm so tired. And I'm resentful too, because I don't have any time to myself. I used to have no other outlet except for my work."

Like many people, particularly those living in New York, she did some soul-searching after the events of September 11, 2001. "I used to think I'm going to get everything I need to get done in my business life, and then whatever time I have left over, I'll figure out something to do at the last minute," she says. "My M.O. for years and years was that I'd get around to a personal life when I had time."

Patrice began working with a personal coach and says it was one of the best things she has ever done for herself. The coach started by asking Patrice about her purpose in life. Patrice found this ironic because she uses the same question on potential new hires, but she had never asked it of herself.

"I thought about it and I came back to her and said, you know, I considered trying for a more elaborate purpose, but I always came back to the feeling that my purpose in life is to have joy in my life every single day."

Now joy is something Patrice looks for every day. "When I wake up in the morning, I ask for joy and abundance in my life, and before I go to bed every night, I count the joyful episodes in my life that day, so I can reinforce the fact that the day was indeed filled with much joy."

Patrice's tally at the end of the day might be six or seven joyful moments or sometimes more than a dozen. "It's little things to big things," she says. "Everything from I had a really lovely and pleasant exchange with a cab driver going to work. Or that a client called and was so appreciative of something the team did."

With the first assignment accomplished, the coach was ready to move Patrice on to the next step. She asked Patrice what brought her joy in life. Patrice's answer was that she loves to dance and that she even had the phone number of a dance studio. "She said, how long have you been holding on to that number? I had to admit it was like a year and a half.

She said, do you think by the next time we talk, you can set up a lesson?" Patrice agreed and finally made the call to book an appointment about thirty minutes before her next coaching session. "That's what's so powerful about coaching," she says. "You identify things you want to do or need to do, and there's a deadline."

Now Patrice is passionate about her ballroom dancing and is actually dancing in competitions. "I love it so much," she says. "I actually take lessons during the day."

At first, Patrice was hesitant to take part of her workday for dance class. Then her dance teacher asked her, "Aren't you the CEO of the company?" Patrice suddenly realized she did have the freedom to schedule herself into the week.

Patrice has also begun to understand that it's not bad for business for her to have interests outside of work. "The beauty of having partners and really good people is that I don't have to do it all myself," she says. "In fact, if you do it all yourself, it can be de-motivating for other people."

And it's certainly good for her sense of well-being. "It makes my life feel more seamless," she says. "Now my challenge is I love my dancing as much as—or more than—my work."

KooKoo Bear Kids:
The Best of Both Worlds—and Then Some

Tara's day moves to a steady (if challenging) beat of now mom, now business owner, now mom, now business owner. She takes all three kids to school before heading to the office and generally is home in time to help with homework in the afternoon.

"I'm almost always home for the kids in the afternoon, but sometimes I'll come back to the office when Joe gets home at night. Or there are times when I have to take my kids with me. Sometimes I'll say we're going to get pizza and go to the office. It's six o'clock and we're finished with homework. They'll watch a movie or something here at the office—play on the computer, whatever they want to do."

Tara's days vary depending on whether it's her week for carpool or if they're in crunch time at the office. To her, the ever-changing schedule is normal stuff. "There's a lot of back and forth [between the office and home]," she says. "I would say I probably put in fifty to sixty hours a week. A lot of it is at night after the kids are in bed. I don't have a structured schedule. But that wouldn't be me."

In the business world, Tara never apologizes for having kids, and as a mother, she feels that her business improves her ability to be a good parent. "I love being a mom," she says. "My company definitely makes me a better mom." Tara says that when she was a stay-at-home mother, she felt she had less patience for her children because she was with them nonstop. Now, she says she occasionally feels guilty that she doesn't spend as much time with them as she'd like, but she feels confident that the quality of the time she has with her kids is better than ever.

Although the kids have to put up with pizza at the office some evenings, and there are periodic stretches when both their parents are spending long days at work, they also know that when they need Tara to be somewhere, she's there. Tara's sister, who doesn't have children, sometimes doesn't understand when Tara needs to drop a work-related task and rush home. At work, Tara is clear with everyone that kids sometimes trump business, and she doesn't like people at her kids' school to think she's not as accessible as any stay-at-home mom. She doesn't want to be categorized as a working mom with no time to help, so she'll often take time out of the office for classroom activities or volunteer projects at the school. "It's very important to me that people in their school community, and the other moms, know that I'm available," she says.

For Tara, that's a big selling point for combining motherhood with entrepreneurship. "That's one reason why I want to be a business owner," she says. "I want to be there for my kids. I don't want to report to any-body. I don't want anyone to tell me that I can't go to my child's school today or I can't go pick them up because they're sick."

Still, as everybody knows, when you're asking yourself to give 100 percent to two full-time propositions, you set yourself up for pressure. For Tara, the times when she has the most difficulty occur when she's in the middle of a long photo shoot or when a new catalog has just dropped. "When photographers are here and stylists are here, you've got to be there. My kids don't understand that. One of us always tries to be home. If I'm in photography, Joe will try to get home at 3:30. That's part of our partnership as well. My sister loves my children to death, too, so she'll even help out."

This past Christmas, when KooKoo Bear did its first gift catalog, the place was jumping with holiday orders. "Christmas was difficult because I was so torn between my family and my business." Tara says that the kids were eager to get the Christmas tree up and decorated, but she and Joe didn't have time. She couldn't break away from the office to go Christmas shopping with the kids, or volunteer for holiday activities at the school.

The kids began to resent her time at KooKoo Bear, but Tara turned the experience into a life lesson. "My middle one, Connor, said, 'Can't you just quit KooKoo Bear Kids?' And my oldest, Ryan, said, 'Why did you start this anyway? You shouldn't have started it, Mom.' That was tough to hear, so I said, 'Tell me what I would do differently if I didn't have KooKoo Bear.' And we talked about it. I said, 'I realize your frustra-tion, and Mommy is frustrated too.' I didn't want to work twelve to fifteen hours a day, they might as well know that, but I had no choice. It's not going to be like this forever. I always tell my kids that if they start a sport, they can't quit—even if they hate it. And that's always my philosophy; you can't quit." The kids understood once Tara phrased the situation that way, and Christmas became slightly easier from that point on. "They were fantastic," says Tara.

Tara deals with having to take time away from her kids during busy stretches by giving them extra time afterward. "During our slow time, we take our children away somewhere fun." After one Christmas, they took a six-day family vacation to binge on quality time. "It was just the kids and Joe and me, and we did whatever they wanted to do. Now I don't feel so guilty because I had such a fun time with them."

Recognizing when the family needs some extra time, and taking advantage of empty spaces in the calendar by actually picking up and going, are key to keeping life on track for Tara. "It's tough to balance quality of life with a business like this," she says. "It's very stressful some days. You have to step back from it and say I need to walk away from it and spend time with my children. That's probably the most difficult thing to remember."

With Joe and Tara working together in their own company, they can take vacations much more frequently than they could if either of them had a regular job with more limited time off. "Our quality of life is better because of it," she says. When they plan a family getaway to take advantage of school holidays or summer vacation, Trace can handle the day-to-day operation of the business.

One thing that makes impromptu trips easier is Tara's strategy of keeping the preparations simple. "I don't get crazy packing," she says. "You've got these moms who have these whole lists planning it out. I never stress about what we have or what the kids have. Literally, we take thirty minutes to pack our bags. We ride a little bit by the seat of our pants."

Eventually, Tara could see selling KooKoo Bear Kids, just as they sold Joe's first company. "If we were to sell the company, I would still want to be a part of it," she says. "I would probably want to work a little less. Maybe come in two or three days a week, on a consultant basis, something like that. Do I want to do that now? No, not at all. I'm not ready for that. I'm too emotionally attached."

Financial Stress Reduction:
Daily Goal: Love Life

In Chellie's world, it's all about enjoying every day. "I love my life," she says. "I really love my life. I do everything I want to do."

Here's how she maps out her workweek. She takes care of her paperwork on Monday mornings. Often she spends Monday afternoons playing poker in a weekly tournament. On Tuesday, Wednesday, and Thursday mornings she works the phone, making sales calls to prospects gleaned through networking. Her evenings are booked with workshops or those never-ending networking events, of which she attends ten or more a month. Afternoons are free. She might watch a little television or even take a nap. And get this: She doesn't work Fridays at all.

Chellie's sales calls follow the cycle of her workshop. "The two weeks before my workshops start are really high energy," she says. "I'm calling all the people who said maybe, to try to get them to sign up for the class. Once the class has started, I give myself a break on the sales calling for a few weeks, and then I start up again six weeks before the next class."

Chellie also takes seasonal breaks when she doesn't teach her workshops at all. She always takes January and June off and has recently decided to add July. "Ever since I graduated from school, I'm not happy if I don't get that summer break," she says. "That's important for work, too. You need to be taking off on a regular basis so that you can be energized and excited to go back."

One of Chellie's pet peeves is people who can't get around to taking a vacation. "People tell me they're rundown all the time and then they think a new career is going to do it," she says. "They're burned out." Chellie tries to help her clients understand that vacations can actually be more productive than working too hard. "I think that's a mistake that people make," she says. "People get driven by fear. They're afraid if they don't work all the time that they're going to lose money, lose business, and that people will forget about them, so they don't take vacations."

She especially sees this with entrepreneurs. "They feel like they've got to go to every possible networking meeting. That they have to talk to every person whose business card they get. Well, you can't do every-thing. It's not possible. You just have to stop somewhere. Take your vacations."

Chellie knows a woman in graphic design who uses upcoming vaca-tions to bring in new projects when business is flagging. "She'll call all her clients and say, 'Listen, I'm going out of town in a week, so you've got to get your projects in before I leave for vacation.' Sometimes when she's slow, she'll do that even when she's not going anywhere," Chellie says.

No one would accuse Chellie of being one of those workaholic entrepreneurs who can never give it a rest. "I live my life my way," she says. "I take tons of time off. I want to work really full out at what I love, but I don't want to go twenty-four hours a day. I've done that pace before and I wasn't a happy person."

Chellie is working on her second book during the mornings, because that's when her mind is clear. She also writes an e-zine that she sends as an e-mail blast to past workshop participants, fans of her first book (*The Wealthy Spirit: Daily Affirmations for Financial Stress Reduc-tion*), and everyone else on her mailing list. But she won't commit to any certain timetable for upcoming issues of the e-zine. "I just don't need another deadline in my life," she says. "So I do it whenever I want to and whenever I have something to say. We're all overloaded with information anyway."

To work at the pace that's comfortable for her, Chellie is purposely not creating a marketing empire. "Maybe you've got a big pot full of money. But to me, the game of life is not dying with the most money in the bank. I don't think I'm really talented at running a business. My work is teaching what I teach."

Chellie prefers to forgo many of the standard revenue enhancers for speakers and workshop leaders. Typically, speakers have books, special reports, videos, and other wares for sale on their Web sites. Chellie feels that incorporating those elements would only create more work for her and she doesn't want that. "People are always trying to get me to invest in products," she says. "I specifically go for keeping it small and staying undercommited so I have a lot of free time."

She's also not afraid to say no to opportunities she judges not worth the effort. "I try not to book speaking engagements outside of L.A. because I don't want to live out of a suitcase," she says. It's important to Chellie to not sacrifice her quality of life for some extra bucks. She recently had a call from a woman who wanted her to speak at an association meeting in Florida but didn't have the budget for Chellie's usual speaking fee. Chellie had no problem turning her down politely. The woman told Chellie that she couldn't afford to come up with even half of the speaking fee. Chellie

instant wisdom
ON THE QUALITY OF YOUR LIFE

Structure your days so you can get the most done with the least effort.

Sometimes a nap is the most productive thing you can do.

You score no points for martyrdom. If you don't enjoy the majority of your days, change something now.

Working hard is a lot more tolerable if you get to choose when you do the work.

When you're the boss, you're the only one who will notice if you work too hard. Work the way you want to work.

Everyone deserves to have a nice day.

held her ground and told the woman that she would not do it for anything less than her usual fee. The woman ended up finding a sponsor and calling her back the next week offering the full amount of money.

Sounds like a successful negotiation, but when Chellie talks about what it takes to pull off a speaking gig, her $5,000 fee doesn't seem like so much. "It's a whole day of flying there, all the schlepping in the airport, booking into the hotel, and then the next day you're on stage all day. You're meeting all these strangers, and then giving your talk, and then being at their party that evening. And then the third day, you spend the whole day getting to the airport and flying again. So it's three days work for $5,000, which is not huge. I mean in one day, I can enroll three people in my workshop and that's $4,500 right there." Chellie is always looking at risk and reward when she's deciding whether or not to do something. She says she is looking for high profit and low effort.

As for what Chellie sees for herself on the horizon, she says, "I'm really living the life I want to be living right now. There isn't a next place for me to have to get to. I'd love to have a bestselling book, but my deal is to be available to the people who want the information that I have. And I am. My people are finding it." ■

❧ **SHERRY ESSIG** is a business coach and co-owner of Priority Ventures Group (*www.priorityventures.com*) in Raleigh, North Carolina. Through individual coaching, seminars, and speaking engagements, Sherry helps people make more results-focused choices in both their business and personal lives.

How did you know it was time to start your own business?
After helping care for one of my closest friends as he was dying, I made the decision to leave my corporate job to take some time off to figure out what I really wanted to do with my life. I realized that I loved the freedom of being out of the corporate environment and decided it was time to try something on my own.

Did it feel like a big risk?
Two weeks before my friend Paul died, we had a conversation where he was trying to decide whether or not to continue his medical treatments. His quality of life was horrible at this point and he was ready to go. It made me realize what it looked like to be down to your last choice in life. So, no, starting my own business did not feel like a risk at that point. Not taking the risk felt much more scary and risky.

Did you have a formal business plan laid out?
No. We didn't actually set out to start a business, but rather to just do a few projects until I figured out what I really wanted to do. A few months into it, we realized that we wanted to turn it into a "real" business.

How long was it until you were able to pay yourself?
We were very lucky and started our business with a large client.

Before you started your company, what were you clueless about?
How to emotionally let go of my mistakes. As in really let go of them. How to just clean them up, learn from them, and just keep moving on.

How do you find your clients?
Primarily through a combination of referrals, my involvement in women's business organizations, and public speaking.

What's your finest wisdom on developing new business?
Be authentic. Be generous. Be prepared. Honor commitments. Learn from every single interaction that you have. Believe in what you do.

What do you read for business inspiration?
Fast Company magazine. *Worthwhile* magazine. Books on personal development because being my best self is often when I'm most inspired.

What do you tell yourself during slow times?
That it's the perfect time to do business development. Slow times are an opportunity to do the things there isn't time to do when it's busy.

What would you tell someone whose business is growing faster than she can handle?
Slow it down if you can. Your reputation is your most valuable asset, and if you can't handle the growth, it will cost you business in the long run. If you can't slow it down, be honest with your customers so they don't get nasty surprises. Seriously consider finding someone who can help you handle the growth.

What's the best advice anybody ever gave you?
Don't be afraid to ask for help.

What's one mistake you won't make twice?
Ignoring my instincts on taking on a client who just didn't feel right.

Whom do you talk to when you need advice or a sounding board?
My significant other, my coach, my business partner, and a handful of friends and colleagues whom I turn to for support in specific areas, depending on their expertise.

What do you like best about owning your own company?
Complete accountability for cause and effect. I make the choices. I live with the outcomes.

What do you like least?
Quitting my job is not an option on the tough days.

Describe your best day and your worst day.

For the best day, it's hard to pick just one. But a few months after I had been the speaker at a NAWBO meeting, a women came up to me at a conference we were both attending and said, "What you said touched me deeply. I really needed to hear it that day. Thank you." My worst day was when I had a client refuse to pay for a contract that we had completed. [This was a client] we'd felt uncomfortable with from the beginning but had ignored our instincts.

Does having your own business give you more or less freedom than working for someone else?

It gives me more of a sense of control. I choose what I say yes and no to. I'm always very clear on why I'm making commitments and choices. For me, that leads to a greater feeling of freedom.

Does your business improve your lifestyle or make your life more difficult?

It has dramatically improved my lifestyle. My life and my business are very integrated and aligned.

Could you ever work for someone else again?

It would be very difficult. I never say never, but it's pretty unimaginable.

What do you think you'll do next?

I can't imagine doing anything other than what I'm now doing. I've found my perfect corner in the universe.

❧ CLAUDIA BROOKS D'AVANZO is founder and president of Creative Communications Consultants, Inc. in Atlanta, Georgia. Her company is an independent public relations "boutique" agency servicing select clientele in corporate, consumer, health care, and not-for-profit organizations.

How did you know it was time to start your own company?

I think I instinctively knew in my twenties I'd eventually run my own show. However, I took the time to invest in gaining substantial knowledge and experience from some of the best PR firms in the world before I made the leap.

Did it feel like a big risk?
Oh, yes.

How much startup capital did it take?
I set aside $10,000 to pay myself for a few months.

Did you have a formal business plan laid out?
No. Just a brief outline—and a lot of ideas in my head. I run the business intuitively.

How long was it before you could pay yourself?
Thankfully, almost immediately!

What's your finest wisdom on developing new business?
Work with excellent people and be selective about your clientele; they say a lot about you. Do superb work, allow your passion to spill over, and your reputation will begin to precede you.

What's the secret to hiring the right people?
Take your time. Hire smart. Remember that attitude is as important as skills. And give them the space to succeed.

How do you motivate or inspire your employees?
I try to keep them constantly challenged. They get to stretch as far as they'll go. Creating a positive environment in which the team can thrive. Other perks: bonuses, benefits, a cool office space, dressing casual when there are no meetings, flexibility, comp time when they're working long hours, and other little surprises now and then.

What's the most difficult thing about managing employees?
Being patient when there's so much to be done! Recognizing that, even in a small business, culture matters. And leadership creates and fosters culture. As business owners, one of our biggest responsibilities is to create and nurture a positive, supportive environment for our team. I have very

smart employees who could easily choose to work at bigger companies that probably pay more, but they choose to stay here. And I think a key reason for that is this is a nice, fun place to work.

How do you know when it's time to fire someone?
When I start losing sleep over the person, that's usually the first sign.

What do you tell yourself during slow times?
Worry only about what you can control. Something else usually comes along.

What would you tell someone whose business is growing faster than she can handle?
It's a crossroads many successful business owners will face. In my case, I opted to stay small. Coming to terms with that decision was a little tough at first but absolutely the right choice.

What's one mistake you won't make twice?
Taking a client just for the money, and taking too long to move on an employee who didn't have the right stuff to make it.

What do you like best about owning your own company?
Freedom to live the life I choose. Freedom to be there for our kids—whenever that may be. Freedom to do work that matters to me. Freedom to work with people I like being around. Freedom to have fun!

Describe your best day and your worst day.
Best day: Drop off happy kids at school; coffee at Starbucks before work with my husband; walk Lucy, our Great Dane; do a few good hours of work in the office; share funny moments and laughter with my terrific team; ride my horses on a warm, quiet afternoon; watch the kids at soccer practice; make a family dinner; and settle in to a nice, quiet night at home. Worst day: Race to drop off unhappy, complaining kids late at school; no time for coffee with Mike; Lucy doesn't get her walk; things go wrong at work; team is stressed out; no time to see the horses; ask someone to take the kids to soccer because I can't; no family dinner; and that night everyone at home is grouchy and fighting.

Does having your own business give you more or less freedom than working for someone else?
More, absolutely.

What do your kids think about what you do?
I think they're both proud of Mom in their own way. However, they don't like it when I'm not as available to them as they think I should be (and they're usually right!). They put me right in my place and show me what matters.

Could you ever work for someone else again?
Doubtful.

Do you have an exit plan?
I don't think about an "exit." But I do think about the next chapter. My idea of retirement is slowing down, handling a few consulting jobs at a time, and sizing down the business when the time is right. Ideally, I'd work half-time doing PR and half-time riding and training horses.

How would a guy run your business differently?
Well, he'd probably crunch more numbers, examine profit and loss statements, do more forecasting and a lot more worrying. I run the business more intuitively, but for some reason the formula works. We've had seven straight years of success!

DENISE JOY EMBRY owns Ella's Room (*www.ellasroom.com*), a 750-square-foot retail store. Among many products, her store features intimate apparel and lingerie, sleepwear, robes, and men's underwear.

Before you started your company, what were you clueless about?
A formal business plan.

Did it feel like a big risk?
No, because I started out very small.

How much startup capital did it take?
$20,000 in 1998.

How long was it before you could pay yourself?
Around four months.

How do you find customers?
I don't; they find me through advertisements and word of mouth.

How did you know it was time to hire your first employee?
I got sick and did not want to close for four days.

What's the most difficult thing about managing employees?
Having to fire them, of course. The good times are easy.

What do you tell yourself during slow times?
Thank goodness my overhead is low!

What would you tell someone whose business is growing faster than she can handle?
I would tell her to look at the growth spurt as a short-term thing and not to make any permanent business decisions.

What's the best advice anybody ever gave you?
Do not try to appeal to everybody.

What's one mistake you won't make twice?
Buying too heavily in the spring when taxes are due and sales are slim.

What couldn't you have done without?
Confidence and a good personality.

What do you like best about owning your own business?
I can bring my dog to work and arrange my own schedule.

What do you like least?
Having to stand my ground with an unhappy customer, i.e., not being able to pass the buck to a higher up.

Does your business improve your lifestyle or make your lifestyle more difficult?
Improves my lifestyle.

Could you ever work for someone else again?
Yes, because my ego is not too big. Ego is key.

What do you thing you'll do next?
Expand into a larger store when the right one comes along.

What's the secret to a successful cash flow?
Bring money in every day, and pay as you go.

Does having your own business give you more or less freedom than working for someone else?
Definitely more freedom!

Do you have an exit plan?
No. I don't need one. My store is very successful.

How would a guy run your business differently?
He would probably rely on the paper history generated by my book-keeper and the history of the store primarily followed by a small amount of intuition. I run on intuition and do not evaluate my paper history.

❧ CELINE SOPRANO is the owner of C...is for Chocolate (*www.cisforchocolate.com*), a chocolate designer and gift-maker. Her store is located in Burbank, California, and her products are offered through the company's Web site.

How did you know when it was time to start your own company?
When I had no more ladder to climb in the company I was working for.

Did it feel like a big risk?
No, it felt like the right thing to do.

How much startup capital did it take?
About $10,000.

Did you have a formal business plan laid out?
Business plan—yes, but not formal.

Before you started your company, what were you clueless about?
Building a Web site.

How do you find customers?
Call, call, call . . .

What's the secret to hiring the right people?
Building a good eye-contact relationship.

How do you motivate or inspire your employees?
Offer excellent benefits and rewards. Thank them.

What's the most difficult thing about managing employees?
Not crossing the line when "personal matters" arise.

How do you know when it's time to fire someone?
He or she seems not to "care" anymore.

What would you tell a friend whose company is going through a dry spell?
Switch gears; create a new product.

What would you tell someone whose business is growing faster than she can handle?
Hire and delegate.

Whom do you talk to when you need advice or a sounding board?
I like to ask customers what they think.

What's the best advice anybody ever gave you?
You won't know if you don't try it.

What couldn't you have done without?
My husband's help.

What do you like best about owning your own company?
I can manage my own time and be creative.

What do your kids think about what you do?
We make chocolates—the answer is pretty obvious!

Does having your own business give you more or less freedom than working for someone else?
I have more time for my family.

Could you ever work for someone else again?
Yes.

What do you think you'll do next?
Get the right exposure; open a retail store.

What do you tell yourself during slow times?
It's a good time to clean up your desk and your head!

How would a guy run your business differently?
A guy would probably hire more people to do what I do: Web site maintenance, decoration . . . ■

He is always right who suspects that he makes mistakes.

Spanish proverb

୧୨

7

How to Be the Boss
Without Being a Bitch

———

Bossing is not something that comes easily to most women. We're too well trained in being nice, too averse to hurting someone's feelings. We don't want anyone to think we're pushy—or, worse yet, a raving bitch.

We do tend to be good at nurturing our underlings, building relationships with them, and picking up on their nonverbal cues. We generally score a little higher than men on verbal communication as well, so employees have an easier time talking to us.

Women may even be better at hiring than men, because we trust our intuitive feel for whether someone is right for the job, but we are far worse at firing than a typical male manager. Most of us hate the idea of terminating an employee, especially since employees sometimes become like surrogate children to us. We watch their growth and try to spur their development. We let them cry on our shoulders when something doesn't work out. How can we fire them? It's like leading a lamb to slaughter. When you get right down to it, what we really want is for everyone to like us—which, unfortunately, is almost always mutually exclusive with being the boss.

When B.A. and I ran MATCH, our employees tended to think I was the mean one. B.A. is just so darn nice, and she doesn't like confrontation, and she also had many more years under her belt of managing creative people successfully. I was much newer at that, and still didn't quite understand that you can't treat the delicate psyche of an artist (or copywriter or broadcast producer, for that matter) with the same forcefulness you might need with a bunch of steelworkers. In retrospect, I think I was modeling my management style on a sitcom version of how to be the boss. Who did I think I was—Mr. Drysdale sniping at Jane Hathaway? Larry bellowing at Darren Stevens? Without realizing it, I guess I was trying to manage like a man, or rather, in the way I imagined a man would do it.

One way to avoid putting yourself (or anyone on your management team) into the bad-cop role is to gather the best people you can around you. If they are people you admire and whose talent you respect, and you also happen to genuinely like them, then the management part becomes a moot point. All you have to do is sit back and let them do their job.

PT&Co.:
They Should Give an Award for This

Out of the many awards her agency has won, Patrice is particularly proud of the one that named PT&Co. the Number One Employer of Choice among midsize PR firms in America. But if one of your three primary business goals is to create a nearly Utopian workplace, then people are going to expect you to be something like the poster child for the perfect boss. Patrice is an extraordinary boss, but it's a goal that continues to stretch her. One thing she's found is that it's easier to be a beloved leader during the easy times than when tough decisions must be made. Sometimes, doing what seems best for the workplace scores you precious few points with the people who work there.

Even during the lean startup days, PT&Co. didn't shirk its objective of providing ample benefits, which is perhaps a reflection of all thirteen employees who held an ownership position. "Our benefits were really good benefits even when we first started the agency," Patrice says. "One of the most controversial things was to have a paid maternity policy from the get-go. But one of our partners was pregnant and she was the sole support of the family. She got three months' paid maternity leave and we continued that [policy]."

The agency doesn't buy into that anxiety-provoking waiting period that many companies put new employees through. "Benefits start on the first day you begin working here," she says. The company offers flextime and paid personal days, which give employees a chance to create a healthier rhythm to their work pace, and the office is closed between Christmas and New Year's. Those benefits, along with their three-month paid maternity leave and other family leave provisions, prompted *Working Mother* magazine to recognize PT&Co. on their list of fifteen family-friendly workplaces in America.

To make sure the office avoids an all-work-and-no-play mentality, the three or four employees who are appointed Cruise Directors plan frequent themed parties, occasional afternoon cocktails, and fun extras such as free breakfast on Mondays. PT&Co. reduced some of those types of perks to try to avoid layoffs when client activity began to slow. "Over the past three and a half years, our business has fallen off a bit," Patrice says. While most companies would have moved immediately to trim staff in response to reduced client activity, PT&Co. worked hard to sidestep that scenario. "We took a pretty controversial position that we were going to avoid layoffs," Patrice says. "We did a lot of things in order to avoid them. The four [partners took] a pay reduction that lasted four years. For a ten-month period, we had our employees take a 10 percent reduction. We cut out perks like the Monday morning breakfasts and some other things. The restructuring was one of the most difficult times."

When the agency was ultimately unsuccessful in avoiding layoffs and was forced to restructure the organization of the company, many employees felt surprised and betrayed. Even though Patrice knows it was essential to restructure to save the agency, it still smarts a little that employees don't quite see it that way She accepts that she'll rarely be showered with appreciation for making the difficult decisions. Her approach to dealing with this is to accept that acknowledgment may not occur at all, and what matters to her is that she did what she felt was right. If someone recognizes her efforts, she just considers it a nice extra credit.

Although Patrice shares the burdens of such decisions with her three partners, she feels the weight of the load quite keenly. Perhaps it is because she started the agency as the senior partner and was the one who really pushed to make it happen that Patrice continues to fill the top leadership role.

One thing Patrice has learned is that hiring is best done intuitively, but firing requires quantifying. When considering prospective employees, Patrice says, "We're looking for a person who always goes above and beyond. Somebody who is a problem-solver. Not somebody who's going to spend a lot of time making excuses and complaining or pointing out all the reasons why it may not happen. Someone who can show us, when we're interviewing her, examples of situations where, despite the odds, she didn't take no for an answer, and out of some chaos, came up with something that saved the day. We're looking for perseverance, persistence. People you want in the foxhole with you. Somebody who is always going to make it happen, no matter what."

Firing is a trickier call. Patrice says that their tendency is to give people the benefit of the doubt, although this has often meant letting people who weren't good fits remain at the company long after those around them were convinced that they should go. "We realize that by doing that (which is really just because we don't want to be the bad guy who fires somebody) it's actually created morale problems because the other employees are thinking, What's wrong with these guys? Clearly, this person is not performing. Why is he still here? I am busting my butt and that person is not even doing half as much as I am and they still have a job."

Patrice adds, "The downside of managing like a girl is that sometimes, when we have to fire somebody for poor performance, we somehow feel like maybe we haven't worked hard enough to really train him or give him the skills or give him the resources."

The human resources manager and one owner always sit in on exit interviews, which have provided some instructive conversations. Patrice recalls the exit interview for a woman who had been pressed into a vice-president position, even with concerns on the part of Patrice and the other owners. "We felt that she had that expectation [because she'd been here so long] and that she could make that leap. We really worked with her to make this work. Three years later, it was glaring that it wasn't working. So finally, we had to do something. And at the exit interview, she said, 'I was surprised that they even promoted me to be a VP but who was I to question that.' She felt that her previous level was the level where she could perform well. Frankly, if we hadn't promoted her, then it would have been her decision to stay or leave. She would have been doing a good job at that level without us putting her in the position of being beyond her capabilities."

Those kinds of experiences have really helped Patrice to be more rigorous in terms of work performance. Review conversations are documented and there are follow-up reviews. The entire process has been quantified. Managers inform people when they need to improve, and the message is clear that failure to improve could lead to consequences and possibly termination. Of this type of hard-line policy, Patrice comments, "Saying something like that seemed very harsh before, but it's amazing what people hear and don't hear in a review. Sometimes we've tried to kind of soft-pedal the criticisms, and then they totally don't hear. Now we try to be really clear. Not only do we tell it, we put it in writing. And they have to sign it, so there's no misunderstanding." Patrice says she felt uncomfortable with that at first, but now the people at her company see that it's actually the best way to follow the golden rule. She adds, "We mistakenly think that by pulling our punches and being nicer, playing like a girl, it will be better for people, but it's not. Our HR manager always says, 'If somebody gets fired, there should be no surprise on their part. If there is surprise, then it's a failure of management to have communicated.' But people are invariably surprised."

In the opinion of PT&Co.'s HR manager, being a good manager is not intuitive. He believes what employees expect is consistency and fairness. "Well, that was shocking to me," says Patrice. "And I said, no wonder I suck at this. It's not intuitive."

For years, the standard management practice at her agency had been to treat employees as individuals with their own particular sets of needs. "But what I didn't realize is this person's looking at that person and saying, 'Why is that person getting [special treatment]? Why don't I get that?'" Although she has been open to her HR manager's approach to employee management, Patrice hasn't abandoned her intuitive style. "In part, it's my intuitive response to people and being able to figure out what to do that's helped us do well as an agency and why we're highly regarded as an agency."

One element of the agency's new quantifiable approach to management is a review system based on a numerical scale. They're all expected to score above a certain number. If an employee can't reach that level in a reasonable period of time, that person has to go. "You always want to be on a team with all stars, right? You feel better about yourself and it makes you do that much better," Patrice says.

Patrice is concerned that this new method of evaluating performance might feel onerous to employees, especially after the betrayal many of them felt in the wake of the restructuring. But having this sort of quantifiable measure can actually make employees feel more comfortable. Management is very clear on what it takes to play on this team. "[Employees] know this is the expectation," Patrice says.

"The funny thing is that we set the bar high for ourselves in terms of we're going to give employees this and that, we're going to create a positive workplace, we're going to not take on the wrong type of client, and we're going to resign clients that don't treat our staff well," she says. "Yet [up to this point] we were not setting the bar high for performance of our employees—because we wanted to be nice."

Patrice also tries to keep expectations high for the results of group dynamics, particularly in creative meetings. "It's very fragile, the difference between success and failure," she says. Patrice knows this depends in large part on the prevailing mood in the room. "I've seen people who go in [to the meeting] with the attitude of, 'well, I don't think we can come up with anything. No matter what we suggest, [our clients] never like it.' And when others buy into that attitude, it can be a very dangerous thing. As a boss, you have to set the intention that we're going to come up with brilliant ideas. When you have a group of people who are smart, energetic, creative, and desirous of coming up with creative solutions, then you have a strong shot of doing just that."

Patrice works hard to ensure that her employees have positive feelings about the accounts they're asked to handle. "I want people to feel good about the work that they do so that when they leave the workplace, they're energized and positively charged rather than drained. At the end of the day you don't want to be thinking, my God, I had to do this horrible thing for a horrible client. "We try to make sure that employee values are in alignment with the work they're being asked to do and the company that they're working for. If you can get all those things in alignment, you have a better shot at employee retention, at doing award-winning work for clients, and for being known for doing work that matters."

Doing that award-winning work takes some long days and nights, but the tradeoff is that PT&Co. assumes that employees' personal lives will occasionally infringe on the workday. If someone needs to go to a PTA meeting in the middle of the day, no one looks askance. "I like people feeling that they can be their authentic selves here," says Patrice. "At times, you might have to drop everything and go pick up your kid at school. People shouldn't have to feel guilty about that. It is what it is. But we expect it to be a two-way street. Sometimes it's hard to leave at exactly the same time every day, because there's a deadline and your team needs you or something happens at 5:30."

Employees understand that the arrangement requires some give and take, and they know it should even out over the long haul. "We assume people will bill about thirty-five hours a week," Patrice says. "Obviously in our business, nobody works regular seven-hour days, because of the nature of the beast."

At PT&Co., it's not only understood that your personal life will sometimes interfere with work, but it's also assumed that you won't check your emotions at the door. In fact, Patrice says they welcome emotion in the office, which is certainly something you don't usually hear from a male CEO. People sometimes have passionate outbursts or even cry in meetings. "I don't think anybody here thinks it's unprofessional," she says. Even though all the emotional expression can get a little messy, Patrice finds it to be the price of sustaining high levels of creative juice. "I think that suppressing your emotions means that you can't bring your whole self into the office," she says. "And I think that's what we want people to do, so we have optimum access to creativity."

All this effort to support the well-being of employees is more likely to affect the bottom line in a positive way when what you sell is talent. At PT&Co., employees don't need to make more widgets faster. They need to think up better ideas. Patrice goes back to her earlier example of the thin line between potential success and failure at coming up with a creative idea. "It's the difference between believing that you can and not believing that you can. You can have the same people in the room in both cases and get different results. And the only difference is whether you set the intention that this group can come up with that big idea. Everything we need is right here."

This is where an outsider can perhaps most easily understand how the cushy work life of PT&Co. employees can be a true business asset. If you accept that your success or failure depends on the ability to get that best thinking out of your employees again and again, then it makes perfect sense to do everything in your power to enable employees to operate at their highest levels.

KooKoo Bear Kids:
The Opposite of Micromanagement

Tara has clear ideas about the way she wants employees to treat her customers, but she would make a lousy control freak. "I'm very low key," she says. "Not a micromanager at all."

Tara is keen on customer service, but she lets her reps develop their own style. "I'm not real structured on what you have to say," she says. "I always want them to say, 'Thank you for calling KooKoo Bear Kids.' And I want them to act like they're talking to a friend. I would never stand over a rep and say, 'Here's your script of everything you should say to this customer.' But I want employees to treat people like I would treat them. And I think that's a hard thing."

A few months after the first catalog mailing, Tara, Joe, and Trace took on their first non-family employee. The woman, a mother, is still with the company, but she has cut back from working full-time to three days a week. This is an example of the kind of flexibility Tara provides.

The company is now up to eighteen employees—most of them mothers—some of them full-timers and others part-time. "I like having moms," Tara says, "because they can relate to my personality. They know what it's like to juggle. They know what it's like to have the kids wake up one day and they're in a good mood. And another day, the kids wake up in an awful mood and want to wear their pajama shirts to school. What are you going to do?"

You get the feeling that if one of her employees woke up one day and felt like wearing a pajama shirt to work, Tara would be cool with it. "I think I run my business that way, too. You know what? If that's what you want to do, I don't want to fight you about it. That's what I do with my children. Don't fight them on the small stuff."

The accepted attire at KooKoo Bear Kids is business casual, with the emphasis on the casual part. "I don't have a dress code," Tara says. "If you don't feel good and you want to come in your sweats, I don't care. I'm not picky about things like that. If you want to take lunch with your husband, or if you want to go to your kids' preschool for two hours and then come back, that's fine. Unless we're in a catalog drop and it's serious. That's when I want everybody to be here."

There is a rhythm to the pace at KooKoo Bear, and of course it's based on the phase of the catalog. If they've just mailed a catalog, then it's all hands on deck and you might as well cancel that manicure. But during the lull between one catalog and the next, Tara is not uptight about what time her employees show up. "During the holidays, they all work ten-hour days, sometimes twelve-hour days," Tara says. "But they know that come January 1, they can take off whatever time they need."

Tara's employees can take for granted that they don't have to apologize for being parents, or for the inevitable workday snags kids sometimes create. "My girls all know that if you ever have a child you need to bring here, you're always welcome. We have a TV and a sleeping bag, toys, the whole thing. There's plenty for them to do and Mom can still come to work. I'm big on that. Most corporations aren't going to let your children come with you."

When it's time to hire, Tara has some clear ideas about the sort of person she's looking for. "I look for creative people and people who have experience in this business because of the hustle and bustle and juggle of it. I like retail experience; it's valuable."

Tara also looks for people with that innate ability to make friends with the customers. "Here you're on the phone selling somebody but you're still developing that rapport, being a friend with that person just like you are in the store," she says.

Tara says that she looks for good conversationalists rather than computer experts. The computer system they use is easy to learn. She has employees spend a couple of days on a self-training program. Then they shadow a seasoned customer service rep for a while. She also does hands-on training with the merchandise. "Before a catalog is mailed, I do full product training. I want them to feel and touch and see, so they know everything about it. When a customer calls and asks about something, I don't want them to say they don't really know what it looks like."

When hiring for jobs besides customer service representatives—for instance, the position of her assistant—Tara looks for other attributes. Tara admits that she has hired poorly in that position before, but is thrilled with her current assistant, who seems to have an appreciation for all that Tara is trying to balance. "The thing I love about her so much is she respects me," Tara says. "She understands I have to run home for my kids at three o'clock and I'm not coming back. But I'll call her and tell her a whole bunch of things that I need her to do." Tara has had assistants in the past who didn't quite understand that approach. She chalks it up to the fact that they didn't have children, so it was difficult for them to understand the pressures of motherhood, much less the pressures of a mother in charge of a business.

Occasionally, a potential hire is looking for the sort of structure that Tara is loath to provide. "My company is not for those people," Tara says. "Basically, I say to them, I can't be what you want me to be so you should move on. There are plenty of other people who could fill this position."

Tara cringes at the thought of having to fire anyone. "That's a very hard thing for me to do," she says. "I have a tough time with it. Have I? Yes. It hurts me. I don't feel good about doing it. The hard part is that I get very involved with my employees. Firing someone is my worst part of having my own company. It's a hard thing to say to somebody. You like the person, but you have to tell them, 'You're not right for us. We're not right for you.' Which is usually how it is; it's both ways. It's not just they're not right for me. I'm not right for them either."

Fair warning to anyone applying for work at KooKoo Bear Kids: When you're working at a catalog company that's owned by parents, and staffed by parents, and that sells children's products to parents, understanding what it's like to have kids is clearly part of the job.

Financial Stress Reduction:
No Employees? No Problem!

Chellie's solution to issues of employee management is short and sweet: Just skip it. She prefers the simplicity of being on her own and not worrying about funding anyone else's paycheck. "I've found I'm just much happier this way," she says. "When I had the bookkeeping company and I had as many as thirteen employees, I worked for them. That's the thing about employees. You work for them." Chellie says that the best piece of advice on hiring and firing she ever received was, "Hire slowly and fire fast."

Back in the days of her bookkeeping service, Chellie was once burned by one of her employees. "My head bookkeeper decided that she wanted to go into business for herself," she says. "This woman was a talented woman and really knew how to do bookkeeping and she [had a way] with customers. But she didn't like me. I thought I couldn't just fire somebody because they didn't like me. Well, now I know that you can and you should." Several of Chellie's clients walked along with that employee, and became the first clients of the former employee's new company.

As Chellie rebuilt her bookkeeping firm and eventually struggled through hard times with that company, she noticed that many successful people had switched to a different business model. Home-based consultants seemed to Chellie to be less stressed and more relaxed. "They just seemed so much happier," she remembers. "And they kept looking so peaceful and contented. So I kept filing that away in my consciousness."

Chellie's reluctance to take on employees doesn't extend to sub-contractors, however. She's a huge fan of delegating, and even delegates her company's bookkeeping. "I am perfectly capable of doing the book-keeping myself, but I am wasting my energy doing bookkeeping. That is something somebody else can do."

The traditional wisdom often provided to small business owners is that you'll find yourself doing almost everything. Many entrepreneurs assume that they can't afford to pay someone else to do something they could do on their own. But Chellie's thinking differs. If she knows that hiring outside help will cost an extra $200 a month, and the money is not in the budget, she will either find a way to create that $200 or pull the money from another budget category. Even when it's not clear that the money is available, she'll sometimes pay to delegate a task. "You just have

instant wisdom
ON MANAGING PEOPLE

Sometimes doing something well requires doing it poorly at first. If managing people doesn't come easily to you, hang in there and keep learning how to do it better.

The willingness to admit you were wrong or to offer a simple apology can be the most useful assets a boss can have.

Some companies don't need employees. In some cases, you might be better off using subcontractors or freelancers or even other vendors to get things done.

Firing is not fun. Keep that in mind when you're tempted to rush into hiring a potential employee.

Giving employees the flexibility to deal with whatever comes up in their personal lives can sometimes earn you more loyalty than a big fat pay raise ever could.

to do it anyway and know that you're creating space and time in your day to allow you to be more productive and produce more income," she says.

That assumption paid off for Chellie, in the case of handing off her number-crunching. The first time her bookkeeper came, she spent five hours working at Chellie's desk, and Chellie sat on her bed upstairs making sales calls. In that five hours, Chellie signed up two people for workshops. The day's cash flow included $2,400 coming in for those two workshops, and only $200 out to the bookkeeper. She doesn't always use the bookkeeper's day for sales calls, though. "The second time she came, I took a nap while she was here," Chellie says. "That helps, too, because I need to rest. I can't go full-bore all the time."

Chellie makes the decision to delegate based on what she feels she is not the best at. "Also, I delegate the stuff I don't want to do or that's not cost-effective for me to do," she adds.

The big notebook of materials she gives to the twenty participants in each of her workshops is another example of successful delegating. She drops off her 200-page master document at a copy shop nearby, orders the empty binders to be shipped directly to them, and then they output, collate, and assemble the whole thing.

Chellie has recently added an extra workshop each week to her schedule and she is working on the manuscript for her second book. All of this is keeping her busy enough that she might have to consider hiring an employee to help. "There may be a time when I have to do that," she says. "Even now, were I to hire an assistant—which sometimes looks like it might be a good idea—then I would have to make sure I have enough work for the assistant. Your nut becomes bigger—your operating expenses go up because you have to cover that salary." Chellie continues to enjoy the flexibility she has because she keeps her expenses so low. "If I bring more money in, I spend more money or I bank more money. So my life is more fluid and for my personality, this just works better for me." ∎

❧ **KIRSTEN BASELEY** is the vice president and a partner in GAVI International (*www.gavi-international.com*), a full-service marketing communications firm in Barrington, Illinois.

How did you know it was time to start your own company?
When I could no longer muster up the energy to go to work with a smile on my face.

Did it feel like a big risk?
Honestly, I felt so downtrodden from my previous situation that it felt like no risk at all.

Did you have a formal business plan laid out?
Not really, just a solid new client and twelve years' worth of experience in the marketplace.

How do you find your clients?
Mostly by word of mouth, but we also have direct mail campaigns and make cold calls.

Before you started your company, what were you clueless about?
The amount of time HR issues require (payroll, insurance, vacation, sick time, personal days, etc.). These items take up so much time and if you are a small company and do not have an HR person—it's very time-consuming!

What's your finest wisdom on developing new business?
Maintain a flawless reputation and continue to add new programs to your professional portfolio. Then, the only challenge you will be faced with is getting in front of new business prospects. Once there, your reputation and work quality will lead the way.

What's the secret to a successful cash flow?
Invoice your projects immediately upon completion; develop realistic terms that work for both your client and your company, and follow up on outstanding receivables in a timely manner. Provide any information your client needs in order to approve the invoicing immediately.

When did you hire your first employee?
Immediately. We were fortunate to have active business the day we opened our doors. The work simply cannot be done by one person; delegating is key.

What's the secret to hiring the right people?
The ability to identify a problem before you hire someone. Test the person's response timing and communication skills. Present a stressful situation to the person to evaluate his or her reaction.

How do you motivate or inspire your employees?
Keep them involved in as many aspects of the business as possible. Employees love to be on the front line and they should be. That's how they grow. They will feel a sense of ownership and pride if they see the fruits of their labors directly. Introduce them to clients, take them to shows, and send them to training sessions. Don't isolate them and expect them to just follow your lead. Allow them to take ownership, manage, and troubleshoot on their own. But at the same time, maintain some type of internal safety net for them.

What's the most difficult thing about managing people?
Growing their skill levels. People get comfortable and like to do what they know. The challenge is to get them comfortable outside their comfort zone and this will ultimately add a new level of dimension to them and your company.

How do you know when you have to fire someone?
When the person is a disruptive personality within your organization and doesn't get things done consistently and in a timely manner.

What would you tell someone whose business is growing faster than she can handle?
Try as hard as you can to manage the growth without sacrificing quality. Train people and get them involved in your business immediately. Don't let the new hires just fend for themselves. Work together with them and train together. They will have a better understanding of your business, your management style, and your customers' needs.

What would you tell a friend whose company is going through a dry spell?
Get busy. Make calls, go to trade shows, send out letters, join organizations, and create some internal energy. Tell everyone on staff to be on the hunt for business and pursue every option presented to you.

What do you like best about owning your own company?
I answer only to my clients and I no longer have to answer to a boss.

What do you like the least?
Identifying and juggling all the various personalities who make up the organization. It can be very challenging.

What do you read for business inspiration?
Trade journals, *BusinessWeek, Time*, and I always have a book in the works, too—usually a biography on a president or other impactful individual.

What's the best advice anyone has given you?
Learn to listen and don't be afraid to ask for the order.

What's one mistake you won't make twice?
Overpromising on deliveries. It is best to be up-front about timing, even if you disappoint the client before the project begins. That is easier than disappointing them in the end.

What couldn't you have done without?
My business partner. I am in a partnership with a wonderful gentleman. He and I have always said, "What he/she doesn't know, I know. And we can cover all the bases with that knowledge." When you have someone to bounce ideas off, it takes a lot of pressure off you. We have mandates in our company where we always check and balance each other. It is a good combination.

Does your business improve your lifestyle or make your life more difficult?
It definitely improves my lifestyle. One can always acquire more things, but at the end of the day your overall happiness, good health, and your friends and family are the most important things.

Could you ever work for someone else again?
I love the freedom being a business owner allows. But, yes, I could if I had to. I don't mind following another leader, if that person is the right one.

What do you think you'll do next?
Continue on this same path and pursue new business with more vigor. Training people to manage the existing business to my standard will be my next challenge.

Do you have an exit plan?
Not yet, but it is looming in my brain. [It] is a very rough exit plan I'm thinking about, but it wouldn't be for years to come. I love my job too much.

How would a guy run your business differently?
Probably with a heavier hand and less patience for client and employee needs.

MARY S. MOORE is the president, owner, and founder of The Cook's Warehouse (*www.cookswarehouse.com*), a premier gourmet store and cooking school.

How did you know it was time to start your own business?
I just knew; I felt it to the bottom of my toes.

Did it feel like a big risk to start your business?
Oddly, it didn't. I felt like I was young enough that if it didn't work I could recover and do something else and if it did work, I'd be that much better off. Ignorance is sometimes a gift.

How much startup capital did it take?
$150,000.

Did you have a formal business plan laid out?
Yes.

How long was it before you could pay yourself?
Two years.

Before you started your company, what were you clueless about?
What I was getting myself into.

How do you find clients?
Grassroots marketing; know your target[s] and go after them.

What's your finest wisdom on how to gain new business?
[Always] provide great customer service so that you generate repeat business and new business from referrals. Word of mouth is the best and least expensive way to grow.

What's the secret to a successful cash flow?
Keeping a close eye on fluctuations and responding quickly.

How did you know it was time to hire your first employee?
I couldn't do everything.

What's the secret to hiring the right people?
Being patient and not hiring out of desperation—listen to your gut!

How do you motivate or inspire your employees?
Incentives/bonuses/rewards.

What's the most difficult thing about managing employees?
Knowing how to effectively manage each one. Personalities are so different and what works for one does not work for all.

How do you know when it's time to fire someone?
You don't feel good in [his or her] presence.

What would you tell a friend whose company is going through a dry spell?
Look at every aspect of the business and freshen it up.

What would you tell someone whose business is growing faster than she can handle?
Don't be afraid to rely on others and slow down a little if you can.

What's the best advice anybody ever gave you?
Ask for everything.

What is one mistake you won't make twice?
Signing a bad contract.

What wouldn't you have done without?
My friends, family, and lots of faith.

What do you like best about owning your own company?
The constant challenge and learning.

What do you like least?
The HR troubles.

Could you ever work for someone else again?
I don't think I'd want that full-time. I'll always do my own thing.

What do you think you'll do next?
My plan is to continue growing my business. Eventually, I will sell it and then I'll probably start another business.

How would a guy run your business differently?
I think a guy would run my business more black-and-white. My business is high-touch and I think a high level of sensitivity to customers, product selection, feel, etc., is really important. A guy might run it more rigidly.

ॐ **SARA WASKUCH** is the owner of Fleur de Lys Floral & Gifts, LLC (*www. fleurdelysfloral.com*), in New Haven, Connecticut. Her full-service florist and gift shop does environmental and event design, servicing both corporate and private clients.

How did you know it was time to start your own business?
[I was] totally discontent working for others and not doing what I wanted to do.

Did it feel like a big risk?
Yes, lots of heart-pounding and sleepless nights. But I had lots of support from my husband and friends—they kept me grounded, focused, and gave me lots of encouragement.

How much startup capital did it take?
$75,000.

Did you have a formal business plan laid out?
Yes.

How long was it until you could pay yourself?
After four years, I am still not taking a paycheck.

Before you started your company, what were you clueless about?
Hiring people, and how many hours a week I would have to work. It's like having a baby—24/7 for the rest of your life.

How do you find clients?
1. Networking
2. Word of mouth
3. Advertising

What's your finest wisdom on developing new business?
Know your market: Who are your customers and what's the best way to reach them?

What's the secret to a successful cash flow?
Keep up with the paperwork and watch expenses. Stagger expenses to match revenues.

How did you know it was time to hire your first employee?
I couldn't work any more hours! I couldn't handle the load on my own anymore and my business was beginning to suffer for it.

What's the secret to hiring the right people?
Wish I knew! I have been putting all new employees on a six-week "tryout" period before permanent hire and I still make mistakes.

How do you motivate or inspire your employees?
Bonuses and time off.

What's the most difficult thing about managing employees?
For me, I tend to give away my power—always trying to be diplomatic and making everyone happy. In the end, I end up unhappy because my needs are never met.

How do you know when it's time to fire someone?
When the person shows a lack of respect for you and doesn't enjoy what he or she is doing. Discontent and misery loves company—get rid of the virus before it infects everyone else!

Who are your role models?
Martha Stewart, Ina Garten, Hillary Clinton—strong women who know their mind and forge forward no matter what befalls them.

What do you read for business inspiration?
Books by successful business owners, marketing books, and style and design magazines.

What do you tell yourself during slow times?
Get out and market yourself! Be patient; every business has its ups and downs.

What would you tell a friend whose company was going through a dry spell?
Hang in there; get some advice—brainstorm with professionals.

What would you tell someone whose business is growing faster than she can handle?
Get all the advice you can from people with lots of experience in your field or business. Experience is definitely the best teacher.

What's the best advice anybody ever gave you?

Learn every aspect of your company. Be sure you can do every job because there will be a time when you will have to and you want to know everything. Don't be held hostage by anyone or any circumstance—this also helps you to plan, and make more informed decisions.

What's one mistake you won't make twice?

Hiring family, friends, or friends of friends.

Who do you talk to when you need advice or a sounding board?

Other business owners. I have two close friends who own their own businesses and we spend lots of time bouncing things off of each other.

What couldn't you have done without?

The support—emotional, physical, and economic—from my husband.

What do you like best about owning your own company?

The total satisfaction you feel from the accomplishments: You created it—no one else—you own it!

What do you like least?

Without a doubt, managing people.

Describe your best day and your worst day.

Best day is when orders are flowing in and everything falls into place. Worst day is when the delivery van breaks down, someone is out sick, the computer printer goes down, the cooler konks out—and all this always seems to happen the day before a major holiday and we're swamped!

Does your business improve your lifestyle or make your life more difficult?

Both. It did improve my lifestyle in many, many ways, but I never seem to have enough time to do everything I would like to do, so that is very frustrating at times.

Does having your own business give you more or less freedom than working for someone else?
It's a give and take. Sometimes I can just take a few hours or a few days to myself, but during holidays and busy times you work eight days a week!

Could you ever work for someone else again?
Possibly. But it won't be easy—once you are your own boss and you are calling all the shots, it's very difficult to give up that power.

What do you think you'll do next?
Retire; write a book.

Do you have an exit plan?
Yes, working on it.

How would a guy run your business differently?
He would probably be more of a "boss." I find that difficult to do. I started my own business to get away from all that nonsense and it's not easy being on the other side of the table. I have a newfound respect for any manager who can get people to do their jobs and have things run smoothly.

JODY HOUGHTON is president and owner of Jody Houghton Designs (*www.jodyhoughton.com*), Inc. in West Linn, Oregon. Her company designs and distributes greeting cards and gift accessories, including T-shirts.

How did you know it was time to start your own company?
When I was living in Boston, out of work, and wanted $500 for airline tickets to visit my home in Oregon.

Did it feel like a big risk?
No, I let my business grow itself. The profits went back into the business.

How much startup capital did it take to start your company?
Maybe $500 for materials only. I started in the spare bedroom of my home.

How long was it until you were able to pay yourself?
Immediately. I started with arts-and-crafts shows in church basements. Cash and carry is a startup blessing!

Did you have a formal business plan laid out?
Yes. My former career was with state government. Part of my job was to formulate and manage a small state agency budget. Costs and planning [came naturally] after that experience.

What's your finest wisdom on developing new business?
Show up! Go to trade shows, find good sales reps.

What's the most difficult thing about managing employees?
Separating social talk with business functions. As my grandfather used to say, "Girls, a little less jaw work, and a little more paw work." And we were only shucking peas!

How do you motivate or inspire your employees?
Try to involve them in the overall plan of a project, and let them see the bigger picture.

What's your secret to a successful cash flow?
Merchant credit cards.

What's the secret to hiring the right people?
The right person shares your values and product interest.

How do you know when it's time to fire someone?
When the person thinks that a ringing phone is a nuisance rather than an opportunity.

What would you tell someone whose business is growing faster then she can handle?
Breathe deeply and concentrate on your business systems: production, distribution, inventory. Enjoy the ride. Stay in the moment!

What's the best advice anybody ever gave you?
Keep the end in mind. Don't lose sight of your mission.

What's one mistake you won't make twice?
Turning my distribution over to an outside company.

Whom do you talk to when you need advice or a sounding board?
Everybody who will listen. When I hear myself explain the situation, I usu-ally hear my own answer. I also have a business friend twenty years my senior whose advice I value.

What do you like best about owning your own company?
The flexibility of blending family life with business life.

What do you like least?
Not being taken seriously because of my home-based setting.

How has having your own business affected your relationships?
I'm divorced after twenty years. I honestly feel that he was jealous of my success, joy, and balance. It was my deepest loss.

What do your kids think about what you do?
Now that they are twenty-six and twenty-two years old, they finally realize that Mom does have a real job.

Does your business improve your lifestyle or make your life more difficult?
I love my work. I am truly blessed to be working in an area that is actually my passion and element of play. My work brings me joy; I love to share my gifts with others.

Does having your own business give you more or less freedom than working for someone else?
More freedom. One of the main reasons I developed my home-based business was to be with my children and attend their school activities with my full attention and to truly participate in their lives.

Could you ever work for someone else again?
Yes, if I truly felt that I would be learning and contributing.

What do you think you'll do next?
Design, design, design. Less time with day-to-day management and distribution.

Do you have an exit plan?
I was planning on licensing more of my designs and manufacturing/distributing less over the next few years. However, I have learned that licensing is a long-range plan and the manufacturing is a more secure income source.

How would a guy run your business differently?
I don't believe that a man would have been as patient with the growth of my business. Men are usually more competitive with themselves. I worked with a very different mindset about business growth. I let my business grow with the ages of my children. We have always worked "A.M. school bus to P.M. school bus." My business motto is: Creating a Life, While Creating a Living. ∎

We do survive every moment, after all,
except the last one.

John Updike

∾

8

What Doesn't Kill You
Makes You Stronger

———

Every business has cycles, just like in nature, the global economy, the moon, planting season, and hormones. The only thing you can count on is that things won't stay the same. What you hope, as a business owner, is that your up cycles will last longer and reach higher and your down times are short and not too severe.

Starting your own company entails a high level of risk, and you're fooling yourself if you think it doesn't. According to the Small Business Administration, more than 50 percent of small businesses fail within the first year and 95 percent fail in the first five years. Business involves risk and risk includes the very real possibility of failure. But failure doesn't always mean the end of the world, or even of your company.

Many businesses survive some major setbacks along the way. You might hit a stretch so rocky, you're not sure you'll make it through. But if you live through it—and you probably will—you may find that rough stretch provided you with experience and wisdom you wouldn't trade for anything.

You might even look at it this way: Success breeds complacency. If you're looking for a challenge, impending failure is just the ticket.

After a stunning first few years in business, MATCH sustained three heavy blows in quick succession. The first was that MATCH's largest client, our beloved and sacred cash cow, filed Chapter XI. We were in L.A. on a television shoot for that client when it was announced, and I remember feeling smug about having insisted they pay for the commercial production in advance. I had no idea at the time how severely the loss of that client would rock our world. Especially since our second biggest client went out of business almost immediately thereafter.

Next, our CPA gave us a nasty surprise. He had been joking for months about how we were making way too much money. What he didn't communicate very clearly was that we were about to be hit with a tax bill more than six figures higher than what we'd expected. The agency's cash situation was suddenly quite bleak.

We had a fantastic staff of people we loved and wanted to keep working there at MATCH. We had pricey leases on three connecting sections of office space, car leases for the management team, and all sorts of expensive perks that would shortly threaten to eat us alive. Like many passionate entrepreneurs, I so closely identified with my company that I sometimes couldn't quite tell the difference between it and me. Thinking about the possibility of my company going out of business felt like considering my own death. We dug in and worked like dogs and somehow managed to win three major accounts before the close of the year. We made our way out of the woods, but those woods had been damn scary.

Not unlike the human body, many companies turn out to be quite resilient. Moral of the story: You don't go out of business in a day, or a week, or even, apparently, in a handful of months. Also, fear of going out of business is a grand motivator. Discover yourself in a similar situation and you may find that you will pitch new business as if your life depends on it. You'll live through it, and with some hard work and a little luck, your company might even begin to thrive again.

The beautiful thing is that it will be very hard to scare you in the future. You'll get bad news from time to time, but it won't get under your skin the way it used to. It's not as if you will want to tempt fate, or even to be challenged in that way again, but you might find that you have a profound appreciation for what you gained through that experience. As they say, imagine how happy you would be if you lost everything, and then got it back again.

PT&Co.:
Being Solvent Versus Being Liked

Patrice has weathered not one but two serious financial downturns in the history of her business. "I had to think about whether or not to participate in this book, because the past three years have been very difficult ones for the company," she says. "We're still going through it, and it's truly been a journey. Some parts of the journey have been more difficult than I ever would have imagined."

Six months after Patrice and her original twelve partners bought back their agency from Chiat/Day, they lost half their billings in fallout from the recession. "I thought, this is horrendous," she says. "We had two choices. We could either lay off half our staff or we could all take a pay cut to avoid having to lay anyone off. We chose to bite the bullet and ride it out. That's what we did, and between January and December of the following year, 1991, we actually grew 100 percent. We were back to where we were when we started the company fifteen months earlier. And after that, we were all really bonded as a group."

When the next recession started taking a toll on billings, Patrice assumed that they would overcome by following the same strategy. "We thought, 'We'll just do what we did the last time. We'll just tighten our belts and focus on rebuilding and once we're through it, the economy will rally and we'll be okay.'"

But she had no idea that the recovery period would take so long this time around. Since the driving force behind buying themselves back from Chiat/Day initially had been to avoid having anyone in their group laid off, Patrice felt strongly about keeping the team together.

Patrice further committed herself to the path of no layoffs in public statements to her team. "I addressed our staff because everybody was nervous. They could see every agency around us immediately cutting staff. I told them we'd get through it with layoffs as a last resort."

Eventually, Patrice found herself in that dismal place of last resorts. "We made other kinds of cuts, including not making any profit. We took many other actions before we got to this point. We reduced the shareholders' earnings, but really in a service business like ours, there's not much you can cut beyond that."

Finally, there was nothing else they could do. It came down to layoffs being the only way the agency could survive. "We had to look at the business as a whole and what we could afford in terms of staff," Patrice says. "It was the first time I ever looked at it that way or had to look at it that way. The alternative was to keep the group together at all costs and then we probably wouldn't be around for long."

When she looked at the staffing in terms of what positions were necessary to the agency's survival, she found herself staring at the possibility of laying off some of the very people who had originally founded the agency. "I didn't feel that we could say this is a workplace community where the layoffs occurred only below the ownership level." Several of the remaining founders were asked to leave, and the current four partners bought out their ownership in the company.

The negative impact extended to staff morale. "To be perfectly honest, there were people who felt betrayed," she says. "They thought this would never be done here. We tried to explain that we could have made cuts early on when every other agency was making cuts, but we chose not to. People hear what they want to hear. It was a misjudgment, because we thought we could ride it through without making any staff cuts, but that wasn't the case."

Perhaps the most difficult part of the whole ordeal was that Patrice was doing everything she could, at some personal and financial cost, to delay the inevitable. Another business owner might have cut staff far earlier and moved on without worrying about it. "We probably wouldn't have the morale problem that we do now if we had not made a statement as bold as 'Layoffs only as a last resort.' Because we did, everybody feels let down and betrayed and I totally understand it. It's frustrating on both sides," Patrice says. She speculates that if they had not set the bar so high for themselves as a compassionate workplace, they would not have left employees feeling disillusioned. But, she says, setting high expectations is the way her company is run.

Setting that bar so high for the clients they work with has often challenged the agency as well. PT&Co. has resigned several clients, sometimes with financial consequences. "Of course, that gets us into trouble sometimes," Patrice says. "Frankly, that's a double-edge sword. Our team gets it; they appreciate it for that moment." But often they are less appreciative when the move affects their paychecks. Patrice talks about when she made a tough announcement to the group. "We said we're going to have to ask you to do something that we've never had to ask in the history of the company. In order to preserve everyone's job here, we're going to be asking everyone to take a 10 percent salary cut, possibly for a year. Now, some people felt that yes, to preserve our jobs, I'm willing to do that. Other people felt yes, we want to preserve everyone's job, but I don't want to take a salary cut." The overwhelming majority of employees accepted the voluntary pay cut; ten months later their salaries were restored to 100 percent.

It's all part of the agency being true to itself, in Patrice's view. "If we want to stand for something and if we want to live the values we truly believe in, then we have to put a stake in the ground," she says. "Sometimes it can be very exciting and uplifting to people here and sometimes their reaction is that management failed to live up to that and let them down, or worse, they feel betrayed."

She mentions that it's probably typical of many women managers to resist difficult decisions such as cutting staff or asking people to take pay cuts. "In terms of the layoffs, the thought that really sustained me was this," she says. "As much as I care about this person whom I have to lay off, it's more important to protect the needs of the group or the company as a whole." Going forward with layoffs was certainly not a decision she made lightly. "For me, business is personal. I'm never going to say 'It's just business,' and therefore not be mindful of the effect that it has on people."

The hard times have made a significant and injurious impact on Patrice, and on the agency as a whole, but PT&Co. is now recovering nicely. Patrice cites perseverance as her strongest suit. "I'm not the smartest or most creative or most talented, but I can persevere longer than I've seen other people," says Patrice. "If they give up too quickly and you're still standing at the end of the day, sometimes you win just because nobody else has stayed in the game."

KooKoo Bear Kids:
If We'd Known Then What We Know Now

When Tara and Joe launched KooKoo Bear Kids, they had no idea what a money pit a catalog could be. They had Joe's profits from the software company he had built and sold, and were willing to invest some capital, but were blissfully ignorant of just how much capital it would take. "The money going into it was crazy," Tara says. She says that they might not have embarked on the venture at all had they known about the voracious startup expenses.

Just how pricey was it? "I thought it would take $100,000," Tara says. "It probably took half a million dollars to get it up and running." What's more, they were throwing more money at it than most catalog retailers would. They were paying roughly $1.50 to $2.00 on production costs per catalog. "Of course that's why we couldn't make any money," Tara says.

That sparked much spirited debate between Trace, the guardian of the creative caliber, and Joe, the keeper of the coffer. Joe wanted to lower the weight of the paper and cut the size of the book. Trace disagreed and felt that would make the catalog look cheap.

Their growing investments into a venture that was anything but a sure thing grew progressively more stressful for both Tara and Joe. "We kept putting our own money into this," Tara says. "It was like the company was just eating it. We started out with the best paper, the best this, the best that. Well, that costs a lot of money." Tara tried to be the peacekeeper between her husband and sister, as the three of them crept farther and farther out on a limb. "It was a very difficult strain on Joe and me," Tara says, "because here Joe had worked so hard to make this money at his last company and we kept throwing more and more of it into KooKoo Bear."

Finally, they made the tough decision to use lighter paper. They also made the dimensions of the pages smaller and cut a few pages.

When you're paying postage based on weight, all of those decisions significantly affect your bottom line. "We had no choice," Tara says. "If we had kept spending at the pace we were spending, we wouldn't be in business anymore. We couldn't be." Looking back, Tara remembers that time as stressful to the nth degree. "It was difficult. There were many nights that Joe didn't sleep," she says. "We didn't pay ourselves for at least the first year. Today, we're still making changes to the book to get it down to less than $1."

Ultimately, they decided to keep going for the same reason they knew they had to cut the expenses of their catalog production: the numbers. "The response rate was so high for the catalog," Tara says. "The actual statistics looked really good." The average dollar amount per order was $150, and the response rate was over 3 percent, whereas most catalogs are closer to 1 percent on response rate. "You look at the numbers and you see that there are some positives," Tara says. "We could make money with this."

The average catalog company doesn't make money for the first five years. KooKoo Bear Kids is turning a profit less than two years into it. Besides a profit, Tara has gained from the experience—"More gray hairs and more wrinkles," she says. "It seems like we could have done something a lot less risky and for a lot less money." But listening to her tell the story, it's clear she would do it again, anyway.

Financial Stress Reduction:
When All Else Failed

Plenty of business owners would tell you that their worst fear is that something out of their control would send them spiraling into bankruptcy. Chellie has not only entertained that fear, she has actually filed bankruptcy and lived to tell the tale.

After enjoying the easy growth of the 1980s and buying the book-keeping company she had originally been hired to manage, Chellie was able to enjoy her quickly won success for only a short time. "I was cock-of-the-walk for nine months," she says. "Then the group of doctors who were our biggest account wrote me a letter and gave me two weeks notice and I was gone." Chellie had to lay off nine people, who immediately went to work for the doctors' group. She was left with a huge office suite, computers, phones, and big loans.

Her biggest bill was the $4,500 a month she paid in rent. So she called a meeting with her landlords and told them the truth. She said that if she had to continue paying the rent then she would have to file bankruptcy and fold the business. "And they said, 'No, we don't want you to go under. How much space do you need and what can you afford to pay?'" They tore up the lease for $4,500 and wrote a new one for $800. Chellie had no idea it was even possible to do such a thing. She says she had always thought, "You have a contract; you're dead." She decided to try the same approach with other people she owed. She offered to pay a small amount every month until she could get back on her feet. "Almost everybody worked with me," she says. In the meantime, Chellie financed what she hoped was the recovery of her business in the all-American way: with credit cards. "A friend handed me a book called *How to Borrow $50,000 on Credit Cards*," she says. "That was my lifeline. I had golden credit. Unfortunately, there wasn't a companion volume titled *How to Pay Off $50,000 in Credit Cards*. I juggled it and I did save my business. I had a lot of debt but I was very hopeful about getting big new clients and having it all turn around."

Unfortunately for Chellie, things went from bad to worse. She was desperate to unload her condo but was unable to sell it for anywhere close to what she'd paid for it. The cash flow in her business had slowed to a trickle. She owed $80,000 on her credit cards and her minimum payments totaled more than $2,000 a month.

"Then I couldn't pay my credit cards," she says.

That's when things got really hairy. Her creditors became increasingly aggressive. "They called every day. I couldn't work. I couldn't build my business anymore. I went to my attorney and I said, 'What the hell am I going to do?'" Chellie's attorney suggested filing bankruptcy. California bankruptcy law at the time meant that Chellie could essentially dissolve all her debt and put an end to being hounded by her creditors. But bankruptcy laws vary from state to state (and even county to county) and are subject to change, so don't assume it's an easy way to wipe the slate completely clean. If you find yourself in a position to consider bankruptcy, make sure you proceed with caution and only on the advice of your attorney.

For Chellie, the idea of filing for bankruptcy took some getting used to. "I was president of the National Association of Women Business Owners, L.A. chapter. I was vice president of my Rotary Club. I owned a bookkeeping service. I was teaching financial stress reduction. How humiliating is that?"

At the same time, Chellie joined Alcoholics Anonymous. "Because my coping mechanism for all of this stress was drinking, and I was drinking every day. I was lying to myself about it," she says. "I knew it. I watched myself do it. One drink became two, two became three, wine became hard liquor." When Chellie suggested to a friend in AA that she might join, her friend said she had been saving a seat there for Chellie. "I said, 'How did you know?' And she said, 'I think it was the time the NABO group went to a spa for three days and you took six bottles of wine with you.'"

The entire time that Chellie was filing bankruptcy and progressing through the AA's Twelve Step Program, she was still teaching her workshops on financial stress reduction. "I was very embarrassed," she says. "Nobody knew about it. For about six months, I didn't say anything." Then, prompted by someone in her class who was facing possible bankruptcy, Chellie shared her story. Because of the positive feedback she received after this class, she decided to incorporate her bankruptcy experience into every class.

instant wisdom
ON SURVIVING DIFFICULT TIMES

The worst thing that could possibly happen often isn't the end of the world. Companies on the verge of going out of business can recover just in time.

If you're in trouble, say so. Many times other people will work with you until you can dig yourself out.

You don't take the company down with one mistake. You can goof up many times and still be hugely successful.

It's not over 'til the fat lady sings. Don't give up too soon.

Difficult times are sometimes when our real strengths emerge. You might surprise yourself.

The reason people say it's lonely at the top is that it often is.

Being the boss does not mean you get to be voted Miss Popularity, but at the end of the day, being the boss is better than not being the boss.

Your employees will have no idea how difficult it is to be in your position and how hard you work at doing the right thing. Get over it.

All you can do is all you can do. Life goes on.

"I had to tell people that this is the reality. You can suffer. You can be broken, you can be in the dirt, and you can pick yourself up and make things better. I believe that I had to go through that experience in order to help others. Everybody hides failure." Chellie has seen how much it helps people to hear an honest account of what she went through and to realize that she's now in better financial shape than ever.

"There's something to be said for experiencing failure and bouncing back to give it another try," Chellie says. "One of my very favorite quotes is that failure is not the falling down, but the staying down. I love that."

The difficult times Chellie faced haven't soured her on running her own company, nor have they made her run for the safety of a steady paycheck. "Everything's a risk," she says. "You have to trust in your ability to make it work. Either on the job or working for yourself. It all comes down to you." ■

℘ **LAINEY HASHORVA** is the owner and an artist for The Magic Bean Company in Los Angeles, California. She designs and manufactures a line of handcrafted gift and home accessories.

How did you know it was time to start your own company?
When I had to quit my day job to keep up with what I was doing on the side.

Did it feel like a big risk?
Yes. But there was almost no choice to it.

How much startup capital did it take?
Approximately $100.

How long was it before you could pay yourself?
A few months.

Before you started your company, what were you clueless about?
The difference between purchase orders and invoices.

How do you find customers?
International trade shows and traveling.

How did you know it was time to hire your first employee?
When I was having heart palpitations from too much work.

What's the secret to hiring the right people?
It's all gut reaction to me.

How do you motivate or inspire your employees?
Pay increases, praise, lunches, and good music.

What's the most difficult thing about managing employees?
Becoming a slave to them.

How do you know when it's time to fire someone?
When the person tries to knock off your product.

What do you tell yourself during slow times?

This too shall pass.

What would you tell a friend whose company is going through a dry spell?

Keep your vision. Do other creative endeavors to unblock.

What would you tell someone whose business is growing faster than she can handle?

Breathe. Pace yourself. Hire people. Delegate. Don't try to do it all. Ask for more delivery lead-time.

What's the best advice anybody ever gave you?

Take a typing class.

What's one mistake you won't make twice?

Being too reliant on one resource or employee.

Whom do you talk to when you need advice or a sounding board?

My mother and other friends who are entrepreneurs.

What do you like best about running your own company?

Being the queen. My time is my own. And I have more pride in what I do.

What do you like least?

It's all self-motivated. A constant treadmill to continue and evolve.

Does having your own business give you more freedom or less?

Much more, but hardly ever any vacations.

How would a man run your business differently?

He'd have more of a handle on the financial aspects, the P&L, the inventory. I'm more artistic.

❧ **CICI COFFEE** is the CEO of Natural Body (*www.naturalbody.com*), an earth-conscious day spa and retailer in Atlanta.

How did you know it was time to start your own company?
When I couldn't find what I wanted in my hometown.

Did it feel like a big risk?
No, I could always waitress.

How much startup capital did it take?
$35K of hard cash and two years of my prime.

Did you have a formal business plan laid out?
Yes; I keep it on my desk for a laugh.

How long was it until you could pay yourself?
Two years, and I was still eating potatoes.

Before you started your company, what were you totally clueless about?
Profits versus cash flow.

What's the secret to a successful cash flow?
Planning/preparing.

How do you find clients?
Building a referral business.

How did you know it was time to hire your first employee?
When I couldn't supply the demand.

What's the secret to hiring the right people?
Knowing what your weaknesses are and looking for them as strengths in the people you employ.

How do you motivate or inspire your employees?
Keeping a career path in front of them.

How do you know when it's time to fire someone?
You give them the chance to do better and they don't try.

What do you tell yourself during slow times?
Take a vacation.

What's the best advice anybody ever gave you?
Don't hire family or friends.

What's one mistake you won't make twice?
Actually three times: hiring family or friends.

Who are your role models?
People who go to bed knowing they accomplished everything they could in that day.

What do you read for business inspiration?
My budget.

What couldn't you have done without?
Creativity.

What do you like best about owning your own company?
Patting myself on the back.

What do you like least?
Patting myself on the back.

Describe your best day and your worst day.
My best day is going to bed knowing that I did everything I could with that day. My worst day is going to bed wishing I had done more.

Does your business improve your lifestyle or make your life more difficult?
Improves it every day.

Does having your own business give you more or less freedom than working for someone else?
Less.

Could you ever work for someone else again?
Probably not.

What do you think you'll do next?
Rest.

Do you have an exit plan?
Yes.

How would a guy run your business differently?
He would hire me.

⅌ KIM GAY is the president and CEO of APS in Atlanta, Georgia. Her company provides specialty medical equipment to the health-care industry. She also was recently appointed by the governor to a state committee on health care.

How did you know it was time to start your own company?
When my income maxed out.

Did it feel like a big risk?
No. I'm a risk-taker.

How much startup capital did it take?
I used my 401(k) savings. It was about $17,000 after taxes.

How long was it before you could pay yourself?
One year.

Before you started your company, what were you clueless about?
How to read an income statement and balance sheet.

How do you find clients?
Associations, networking, word of mouth.

What's the secret to successful cash flow?
Selecting the customers you want to work with.

How do you motivate employees?
Praise and money.

What's the secret to hiring the right people?
Follow your gut.

How do you know when it's time to fire someone?
You first see there are problems.

What do you tell yourself during slow times?
Get up and go.

What would you tell someone whose business is growing faster than she can handle?
Take a step back. Fast is not always better. You may lose customers.

What's the best advice anybody ever gave you?
Stay on top of your accounts receivable.

What's one mistake you won't make twice?
Being the most expensive equipment on the market.

What do you like best about owning your own company?
I know how to perform every job in the company.

What do you like least?
Payroll.

How has having your own business affected your marriage?
I divorced.

Whom do you talk to when you need advice?
A mentor who has been in my industry twice as long as I have.

Do you have an exit plan?
Yes, I plan to sell when the time is right.

How would a guy run your business differently?
He probably wouldn't run it any differently.

❧ **DELIA CHAMPION** is the owner of The Flying Biscuit Café (*www.flying-biscuit.com*), a restaurant in Atlanta.

How did you know it was time to start your own company?
The universe placed all of the pieces in front of me.

Did it feel like a big risk?
Yes. But not giving it a try was not an option.

How much startup capital did it take?
$40,000.

Did you have a formal business plan laid out?
Yes, but it was more casual than formal.

How long was it before you could pay yourself?
Two months.

Before you started your company, what were you clueless about?
Responsibility.

What's the secret to a successful cash flow?
Watch your pennies and your dollars will follow.

How did you know it was time to hire your first employee?
I was spending too much time washing dishes.

What's the secret to hiring the right people?
Spending quality time with an applicant.

How do you motivate or inspire your employees?
Motivating with measurable results = cash.

How do you know when it's time to fire someone?
When the person is not fulfilling their job description.

What do you read for inspiration?
Anything that catches my eye—inspiration is everywhere.

What do you tell yourself during slow times?
Tend to the details.

What's the best advice anybody ever gave you?
It's only money.

What couldn't you have done without?
Help from friends and strangers.

What do you like best about owning your own company?
Freedom.

What do you like least?
When the security company calls me in the middle of the night … because of a false alarm.

Does your business improve your lifestyle or make your life more difficult?
Improve. For sure.

Does having your own business give you more or less freedom than working for someone else?
More freedom when I have a strong team.

Could you ever work for someone else again?
Yes. I would be a fabulous consultant.

Do you have an exit plan?
Yes.

How would a guy run your business differently?
Less intuition.

⚡ **NANCY GILFILLAN** founded ComputerJobs.com, Inc. (*www.computer-jobs.com*), the Internet's leading IT employment Web site, in 1995. She is based in Atlanta.

How did you know it was time to start your own company?
It doesn't matter. If it is in your blood, it will happen sooner or later.

Did it feel like a big risk?
It felt like a big risk not to start my own business!

Did you have a formal business plan laid out?
Planning doesn't create a business, doing does.

Before you started your company, what were you clueless about?
Everything.

How do you find customers?
Everyone either is a potential customer or knows one.

What's your finest wisdom on developing new business?
Treat every prospect like they are the most important. You never know when a small account will turn into a big fish.

How did you know it was time to hire your first employee?
When you stop sleeping.

What's the secret to hiring the right people?
Remember that interviewing is like dating: Whatever you don't like about someone in the first hour, multiply by ten in real life!

How do you motivate or inspire your employees?
Play at work. A pinball machine for stress relief, monthly poetry contests to inspire creativity, off-site outings for team building.

What's the most difficult thing about managing employees?
Remembering that most employees' greatest strengths are also their greatest weaknesses.

Who are your role models?
Anyone who owns and runs their own company, from Bill Gates to the local bakery owner.

What do you tell yourself during slow times?
Take a vacation, relax, reflect, and come back with at least one new idea.

What would you tell a friend whose company is going through a dry spell?
Find out why.

What would you tell someone whose business is growing faster than she can handle?
Slow down and don't assume hiring more employees is the answer.

What's the best advice anybody ever gave you?
The customer is always right.

What's one mistake you won't make twice?
Assuming someone else will do things the same way I do.

Whom do you talk to when you need advice or a sounding board?
The people who work for me.

What couldn't you have done without?
My charge cards! [When my husband and I launched the company,] we were a few years ahead of the "dot-com" rush. No lending institution—small business–friendly or otherwise—would take part in loaning us the seed money we needed to start a real business. One day, after receiving the umpteenth credit card application in the mail, I had a brilliant idea. For the next two weeks, I collected Visa applications from a dozen different banks. I diligently filled them out and sent them all back on the same day. No business plan or financial models required—just my name, social security number, and current address. Two weeks and ten shiny new gold cards later, we had our first "investment": more than $100K in unsecured credit at 0 percent interest for the first six months. I also got that chic new pair of shoes I had been eyeing at the mall all month! We paid it off the first year and ultimately secured $25 million in venture capital funding.

Does owning your own business give you more or less freedom than working for someone else?
Depends on your definition of freedom.

Could you ever work for someone else again?
Only if I could learn something from them.

What do you think you'll do next?
Something completely different. ■

A wise man knows everything;
a shrewd one, everybody.

—Anonymous

❧

9

Cracking the Code on Marketing and Sales

———

There's a popular old saw in marketing circles that goes something like this: "About half the money you spend on advertising will be wasted. The trouble is it's impossible to tell ahead of time which half." With fierce competition in the marketplace, how do customers and clients decide what and whom to buy? It's not always based on numbers and logic; it often comes down to relationships and intuition—two things that women tend to understand quite well.

Let's say a corporate marketing director is thinking of trying out a new ad agency. She might call an agency she used when she was in marketing for some other company three jobs ago. Or, she might ask cohorts in the marketing department of some other company, or her brother-in-law who's in the agency business, or her public relations folks, or someone else she trusts, to recommend an agency or two.

Generally, she'll collect a list of several agencies, and then have each one put together a proposal. She'll review each agency's creative work, consider their strategic strengths and past track records, and then have a meeting to get to know the players in each company. And then, after all that, nine times out of ten, she just picks the agency with the people she liked the best.

So at my second startup, Tribe, our marketing efforts for the most part come down to having lunch with friends. Sales for us means not much more than having the right chemistry with prospective clients when we get the chance to meet them. That's a gross oversimplification, of course, but when you step back to evaluate how new business really comes in the door for us, that's pretty much it. And it is probably true as well for many, many companies in the service business sector.

The truth is, in professional service businesses, the sales cycle often takes years. It's not like owning a grocery store, where you run a sale on chicken breasts and can expect people to come charging through the door today to stock up and fill the freezer. People you met many moons ago might suddenly call one day and hand you their business. A company you identified as a target prospect several years in the past might finally be ready for a company of your size.

Activity often begets action—if only indirectly. Just stirring the pot sometimes can make the phone ring. When B.A. and I started MATCH, our new-business system was based on multicolored index cards. Hot pink cards were for hot leads, yellows were for warm, whites were for cold but interesting. The day we started the agency, we had four or five hot pink cards that we knew were sure things. As it turned out, I don't think a single one of those hot pink cards ever resulted in any work at all. But just by push-pinning those cards to the wall of our office, working our way from hot pink to white, planning next steps on each, we some-how hot-wired the engine of our new-business efforts. The phone would start to ring, but generally about clients we'd never even considered.

If business is slow, start doing something. Anything. You've got to rub up against the people who might need what you have to sell. You can do that with advertising, with PR, by word of mouth, or on a giant blimp floating over the city. But don't wait for people to find you. You've got to make it easy for them.

Keep in mind that customers want to know what's in it for them. You'll have better luck getting their attention if you tell them how you can help them, instead of harping on how fabulous you are. What problem do people have that your company can solve?

Make sure you're fishing in the right pond. It won't do you much good to market to people who have no need for you or can't afford you. Also, consider the approval process and chain of command you must go through to make the sale. Are you targeting the people who are actually the decision-makers for your product or service?

Sometimes the best way to boost sales is to give your stuff away for free. Volunteer to do a project for the charity of your choice, and the exposure (or maybe the karma) could lead to a paying client. Offer free samples of your hot-from-the-oven gourmet chocolate chip cookies outside the revolving door of the office building next door to your shop. Tell your current customers they'll get 20 percent off their next job for any referrals that result in a signed contract.

This brings up a good point. If you need business, ask for help. Let your business contacts know you've got unused capacity. Tell your clients you're looking to increase your billings. Ask your restaurant customers to tell their friends about you. People like to help, especially when it comes to startups. For some reason, people often take a vested interest in helping a new business get off the ground. One key to this is attitude. Whatever you do, no matter how glum your financial prospects, try not to portray yourself as a victim. People are a lot more likely to want to do business with, and send business to, someone who conveys enthusiasm and confidence and excitement about what they have to offer.

The road of an entrepreneur is filled with peaks and valleys, so you've got to be able to take the ups and downs without taking either too literally. When sales are up, enjoy the ride, but also make sure to prepare for possible dips in the road ahead. And when sales are down, remind yourself that you could be on the top of the world again with one phone call, one e-mail, one chance meeting that changes everything.

PT&Co.:
Slow and Steady Wins the Race

For many service firms such as ad agencies or CPA firms, the approach to developing new business corresponds to the cycle of their existing clients. When everyone is working as hard as they can to meet client deadlines, new business efforts tend to fall by the wayside. Then one day, somebody in management looks up and realizes business is slow. A client or two leaves; another client's heavy season draws to a close. Then it's an all-out panic to ramp up the new business program. That generally lasts until business picks up, either as a result of those new business efforts or just because the stars somehow align, at which point the new business activities again fall to the bottom of everyone's to-do lists.

PT&Co. is impressive in the way they've built new business development right into their day-to-day business. They take a long-range view that is executed through a million bite-sized steps that are part and parcel of the annual plan for every single account they have. But imagine the task they were up against when they had first bought themselves back from Chiat/Day and potential clients didn't know them from Adam. "There are thousands of PR agencies in the country," says Patrice. "How do you market an agency with a no-name brand? How do you go and pursue new business if nobody knows who you are? You're selling your track record and we had none."

Still, in the beginning, the partners thought it would be a fairly straightforward process. "When we started the agency, I thought, okay, new business is pretty methodical stuff," Patrice says. "So everybody was responsible for different categories where they had expertise and interest." The partners would each identify prospects that they would want to work for and come up with a thoughtful way to approach each of those prospects, whether at a trade show or by getting them some piece of research that might be relevant. The partners would then meet every two weeks to update one another and share successes. Patrice realized after several meetings of "nothing new to report" that no one wanted to make cold calls.

Instead of beating her team over the head, Patrice stepped back to figure out a better way.

"Part of the problem," she says, "is if you're a no-name brand and you just started the agency, it's really hard to sell quickly in a sound bite by citing your major accomplishments." She decided that they should focus instead on a brand-building campaign for the agency.

Although building a brand is easier said than done, PT&Co. made short work of it with a brilliant and workable plan. They started with baby steps. "We had to begin with things that fit our budget," Patrice says. "There were things that we could afford to do and things that we couldn't from the get-go." They engaged in all types of efforts—from advertising to speaking engagements to publicizing the new business to entering work in awards competitions—and then benefited from the publicity generated by those things. One primary goal was just to be visible at industry gatherings. The group also started a database so that they could send out periodic mailings to communicate what they were up to.

Patrice quickly determined that the agency couldn't afford advertising in the publications that would reach the widest circle of prospects. "My feeling was we didn't have enough money to do general advertising, even in *BrandWeek* or *Ad Age*, but we could probably do fairly significant advertising in PR trade publications for a modest amount of money."

Then PT&Co. did the thing that ad agencies are always encouraging their clients to do: They zigged where everyone else was predictably zagging. Instead of a typical ad with a clever headline and arresting visual, PT&Co. ran ads that looked more like magazine articles. "Rather than showcasing our work and beating our chests about our twenty offices in different cities, what we had was a point of view about our industry and what we were trying to accomplish. So our ads were very different from the other ads that ran in those magazines and they got a lot of attention." Almost immediately, these ads led to invitations for speaking engagements and to join the boards of industry trade associations, so the company's exposure began to snowball. They have continued to build that campaign over the years with ad headlines such as "Workplace as Community," "It's All about Soul," and "Lessons Learned." Each ad is a thoughtful essay on how PT&Co. approaches business.

PT&Co. also initiated a machinelike process for producing awards. "On every account, we have the team start building a case study the first day we start work on that account." Her people understand that the expectation is they're going to generate an award-winning case study from the work they do on an account every year. They can choose to do it for the entire campaign or a piece of the campaign, but Patrice and the partners expect a case study from every account. That is how the agency has managed to win roughly 180 awards. "And of course, if you win awards, it reinforces the idea that you're a creative agency producing results for your clients, and that helps us in terms of getting recognition," says Patrice. "That helped us be named the Number One Most Creative Agency. It's all kind of a self-feeding kind of cycle."

This success also feeds right into Patrice's theory that they need to be top-of-mind with other people in their industry. For instance, if Merrill Lynch approached an agency about handling a project, but that agency was already working with Schwab, it would be a conflict of interest for the agency to accept work from Merrill. With Patrice's approach, the hope is that the agency will refer Merrill to PT&Co. And she passes business on to others in the same way. She doesn't take the sort of competitive view that rules out cooperation with other agencies. "I think there's enough business for everybody," she says. "When we get a referral that isn't quite right for us, then we always refer it to another agency. For two reasons: because we want to be helpful to the person who called us and because we want to refer business to other good agencies."

The management team devotes a good deal of time to maintaining their exposure in the industry. The four partners all have different areas of interest and expertise and so they divide and conquer, each joining the groups that make the most sense for their backgrounds. Patrice says that her company is well known in the PR community, the women's organization community, and the category-specific community.

Belonging to all of these groups may sound like a daunting calendar to maintain, but Patrice says that showing up is something each partner takes seriously. "Some days it's like, 'I can't believe I committed to this,' because we're so busy. But it's really important. You can't go in and out. Because if you give your word that you're going to be there, and that you're going to deliver whatever you're responsible for, then you do it. Yes, we all have client commitments, but at the same time, you've committed to this group of people. We don't want to be known as the people who do great work but never fulfill their commitment to the board."

Some companies let marketing efforts drift along with the ebb and flow of their client activity. To that, Patrice responds, "I don't think you can ratchet it up when business is down. It's got to be a constant all the time because of the way that business leads come in. If you're cold calling, it's almost got to be when they're looking. That's why we really don't make cold calls. When a client is looking for an agency, it helps that they know you and you continue to have good visibility and good word of mouth."

Once they get in front of a potential client, PT&Co. makes it clear that the review process works both ways. "It's a chemistry check," Patrice says.

"We're checking them out. They're checking us out. We tell them that. It's got to be the right fit so that we both have the right to say yea or nay."

PT&Co. is not shy about tossing out phrases like "soul of the workplace," even though some potential clients might be put off by the language. Patrice explains that as part of finding a good fit. "We're not for everybody," Patrice says. "The clients who will work well with us feel comfortable with that kind of thing."

PT&Co. also has an organized approach to finding the clients who will be the perfect fit. They have instituted a committee of seven people, from management supervisors up to partners, which is charged with that task. "It's called the Goldilocks Committee," Patrice says, "and they are working on finding the clients that are just right for our agency. It's so we can get out from under client work and responding to those reactive leads, and target those companies and organizations we really want to work for."

Even the Goldilocks group is expected to make continuous progress—regardless of other work demands. Once a month they meet to evaluate their status and set new goals. Patrice doesn't care whether someone commits to pulling together a gigantic presentation or making two phone calls a day, as long as they follow through. "If it's always back-burnered and you say, 'If I have the time, I'm going to do it,' then it never gets done." The magic to this slow and steady approach is that the many small efforts pile up over time until they reach a critical mass. As Patrice says, "Ultimately, it's going to yield results."

KooKoo Bear Kids:
Buying Your Way into People's Homes

In catalog sales, the name of the game is getting your catalog in as many of the right mailboxes as possible. A Web site is a pull medium; you depend on your customers to voluntarily show up at your site. A catalog is a push medium; you can decide to reach customers in a certain zip code and barge your way through their front doors—as long as you can afford the names and addresses.

The largest players play the game most successfully. The mail order giants and the retail behemoths, from Lands' End to Neiman Marcus, are the favored clients of the premier database companies. The system is based on the scratch-my-back plan, whereby one large marketer sells its list to the database company and is therefore in the club and eligible to buy expanded lists culled from other marketers. The names in this game are well targeted and reasonably priced.

In contrast, a small startup marketer like KooKoo Bear Kids is not invited to swim in that pool. "None of those people knew who we were in the beginning," Tara says. "They really don't. Who were we to get good names?"

Their only choice was to work with a small company that dished up inferior names for a hefty price tag. KooKoo Bear wasn't able to specify factors like "catalog buyers" for their list, which is what companies are able to do with large database companies. "We were paying top dollar for names to the point where it was astronomical," Tara says. "It was almost $50 a name and they weren't even prime names. They weren't specifically catalog buyers."

Eventually, after the company had a few catalogs under its belt, Koo-Koo Bear was able to get the attention of an excellent database company. Tara is still not exactly sure how it happened, but she thinks a friend from the kids' school might have intervened behind the scenes.

They've also come a long way in the production quality of the catalog itself, which is their leading marketing vehicle, followed closely by the Web site.

In addition to cutting costs, they've also brainstormed ways to increase sales. One innovative idea was to launch a gifts-only holiday catalog that excluded the usual heft of furniture and bedding. Not distracted by more functional offerings, customers were able to zero in on the irresistible gift options and bought like crazy. The gift catalog resulted in record sales.

Getting potential customers to click on the KooKoo Bear Web site is a different kettle of fish, and one that's sometimes easiest to stir up through media exposure. KooKoo Bear garnered a good deal of positive attention when they were named one of the top ten Web sites for kids by *InStyle* magazine. Each time a magazine includes them in an article, the Web site gets a flurry of hits. KooKoo Bear garners such media exposure through the efforts of their PR agency. They also use some search engine companies that will drive traffic to the site through keywords. But, Tara says, "We turn search engines on and off, because they're expensive to keep going." Additionally, the company keeps in touch with past customers through frequent e-mails. "We don't do any broadband e-mail blasts," Tara says. "We only send e-mails to our customers who give us their e-mail address. "We'll say, this is your Valentine's gift from us: 10 percent off, or we'll do free shipping or something."

They also use traditional advertising occasionally, and relied on that method more heavily in the early days of the company. They have appeared in the *New York Times*, *Martha Stewart Living* and *Martha Stewart Kids*, *American Baby*, and several other parenting and home publications. "Those ads in the *New York Times* are probably why we have a big clientele in the Northeast. But we had a big chunk of our change going into advertising."

These marketing efforts, along with the blessings of good press, have helped their Web business to grow significantly so that it's now 40 percent of the business, compared to 60 percent catalog sales.

For the most cost-effective marketing, you can't beat word of mouth. Tara knows there's nothing like the power of someone saying to a friend, "That is so cute! Where did you get it?" As Tara says, "Moms know what other moms want."

Financial Stress Reduction:
The Money Is in the Phone

Chellie Campbell has a perfectly easy time doing something that scares many entrepreneurs: picking up the phone and asking near strangers for their business. It's a good thing she's not an introvert, because she also spends a significant portion of her workweek out and about on the town, mixing and mingling at one network event after another.

Chellie always tells people that there are three parts to a business: marketing, sales, and delivery. "Every business is like that," she says. "For me, marketing the business is going and giving talks at networking groups, belonging to networking groups, and showing up places where I'm going to be in the way of people who might be interested in the workshop. Sales means calling and signing up those people whom I met at the function. And then I teach the class. That's it. Life is so simple."

Chellie says that everything else related to business is a time waster. "Everything else is what I call *administrivia*. And people spend all their time doing the administrivia part, checking it off the list. They love their paper, because their paper doesn't confront them in any way. Their paper can't say no."

Sure, but for many of us the rejection that's inherent in the sales process is darn uncomfortable. Chellie looks at the endless world of people and thinks simply that some will want to take her class and some will not. "One of the best explanations of sales I ever heard," she says, "is just not to take it personally. Think of a waitress going around to every customer and asking if they want coffee. Some say yes and some say no. When somebody says no, she moves on. She doesn't run crying to the back room because somebody doesn't want coffee." Chellie realizes that you don't need every prospect to say yes. "My job is just to find enough of the people who want to take the class for me to make a living. Again, it's so simple."

These days, Chellie has graphic designers develop her marketing materials, so all of her communications pieces have the professional look of a much larger company. But back when she had her first workshop, she was not yet to the stage of delegating such tasks. She worked up a simple flier and sent it to people she had met as she networked over the years. A good return would have been 2 percent responses—she received zero.

A lot of people would have given themselves an A for effort and quietly put aside the idea of teaching workshops. But Chellie was now enamored with the idea of teaching what she knew. "So I picked up the phone and started calling the people I'd sent fliers to. I went through the mailing list first, and I highlighted the people who were likely prospects. And so I started calling and I enrolled twelve people."

Chellie has a telephone spray-painted metallic gold in the room where she gives her workshops and she uses it as a prop to preach that "the money is in the phone." But she acknowledges that making sales calls is not something that comes easily to most people. "It's never easy to pick up the phone and sell somebody something," she admits. "You have to be passionate about it. That's the only thing that makes you pick up the phone. You have to really want it. I was really willing to do it and to hear no and to learn how to do it better."

Chellie makes it sound pretty simple, but in reality, it can be tough. If you've sent people a mailing and they haven't responded, how would you go about approaching them over the phone? You have to find a system that's comfortable for you. Chellie's approach after her initial mailing was to call her prospects and ask if they received her flier. Invariably they would say they hadn't read it, so she would launch into an enthusiastic explanation of the workshop and then pull them into a conversation about what benefits the workshop might mean for them. Chellie remembers she once had two women who said they wanted to attend but weren't sure it would be valuable. "They asked if I would be willing for them to pay me on the last day of class and I said okay. I believed in myself and

I thought that they would benefit. And sure enough, they both walked into the last day of class with a check." Chellie now offers a money-back guarantee to all attendees, because, she says, she wants them to feel safe. "If you're not better off financially at the end of the class, I'll give you a refund," she promises.

The entry point for her marketing process now is networking groups. She regularly attends ten or twelve functions a month. "I eat breakfast, lunch, and dinner for a living," she says. She usually comes home from each event with ten or fifteen business cards of prospects. When she shows up at a function, she doesn't just hang out with the people she knows. She works the room the whole time, seeking out new faces and starting conversations. She makes a point to spend more time talking about them than herself.

She says it's easy to get a feel for the ripe prospects from her initial conversations with people and how they react to her line of work. "At some point they'll ask me what I do, and I tell them, and you can tell by their smile or the twinkle in their eye or the questions they ask that they're interested." When she gets home from functions, she goes through the day's cache of business cards and decides which ones go in her stack for sales calls.

She's discovered that the routine of eliminating some prospects is an important piece of the process. "It took me some doing to get to that part," she says. "I used to think that everybody was a candidate for what I did and that everybody in the world could benefit. But there are some people who aren't interested, aren't ever going to be interested, and you might as well not even make the phone call. So I look for those cues when I meet somebody."

Chellie believes a lot of people just don't know how to network effectively. "It cannot be all about you, you, you," she says. "That's a mistake people make all the time."

Her approach to sales is to learn about other people first, and then find an opportunity to help them. "It may be just a free gift that you give at that moment, like a tip or a suggestion or a referral," she says. "Or, the person might say something that lets you know that he needs the thing you do for a living, so you can follow up with that and find out what specifically you can do for him."

When Chellie realizes she's talking to someone who could be a prospect, she never starts selling her workshop in the initial conversation. Instead, she gets the person's card and mentions that she'll call soon to talk more about what they're doing.

Chellie stresses that networking functions are for creating opportunities for business referrals, and not the place to pitch your wares. Occasionally, she finds herself at networking functions where people are not well educated about how to network effectively. "They think it's all about the sale," she says. "Sometimes I've been talking with a group of two or three people, and we're having a little conversation, and somebody will come up and say, 'Excuse me for interrupting but I just wanted to give you my card.' Then they hand their card to three people and disappear. It's too self-serving. Nobody's interested."

To connect with sales prospects, Chellie recommends doing the same thing your mother always told you: Be yourself. "Treat every person as if this could be a new friend of yours." She also recommends asking the same sort of questions you'd ask on a first date. Look for common interests or backgrounds or goals. Her most crystallized gem of advice on networking: "Pretend at every function that it's your home and you've invited all these people. You're the hostess. Then it makes reaching out your responsibility."

Another point Chellie stresses is to make sure you're putting yourself in front of the right people. You need to know the demographics of the people who need you. She explains with the following example: "If you're selling lawnmowers, you might go to the gardener's association meeting. But you're probably not going to be attending the movie moguls meeting because they don't buy lawnmowers. They don't mow grass—they have that done. You're also not going to go to the condo homeowner's association because they don't have lawns. I see a lot of times where people are networking in a room where their target market doesn't exist."

Beyond the basic demographics, she recommends paying attention to your gut feelings about a group. "You need to really scope it out in terms of an overall feeling," she says. "You need to get intuitive. Some people want to sell the hard-to-sell customers. I had a guy once in one of my workshops and I said, 'It sounds like you're working too hard to get that customer.' He said, 'But that's the challenge and that's the fun.' I told him that I don't want challenge in my money. I want money, easy and fast. I get my challenge in my poker game. I want to sell to the people who are most likely to want me."

Often, Chellie introduces herself to a new networking group by first appearing as a speaker. She says that lets people get a sense of who she is and then anyone who is truly interested will approach her to talk.

When she calls people to follow up after a speaking engagement or networking event, Chellie still doesn't come out of the gate selling. Instead, she turns the conversation to the other person and his or her business. They're usually pleased to hear from her because she's calling to learn more about them and what they need.

"At some point he's going to ask me about that workshop. I never answer him then. I say, 'Let me ask you a question: What would you change about money in your life?' And because he's been answering my questions for fifteen minutes, he answers that one, too. As personal as it is, he'll say, 'I've got credit card debt,' or 'I need more clients.'" Chellie will then tell him some success stories about the people in her past workshops.

Chellie has learned the hard way that a verbal commitment means nothing. Now she uses a skillful sales technique to get them to put their money where their mouth is. "I give them a choice. It's 'Do you want to come Monday or Wednesday?' It's not 'Do you want to come or not?'

because that's too confrontational. And then we move right on to 'And how would you like to pay for that? Credit card or check?' Again, they're making a decision, not yes or no, but how."

The people who attend Chellie's workshops are mostly entrepreneurs. One of the things she teaches them is to give themselves a raise every year. "If you were working for somebody else, wouldn't you want a raise and promotion?" she asks. "Make more money, charge more money."

She doesn't just talk the talk on that one, either—she does it for herself too. Since she first started her workshops she has steadily raised the price each year, with the net result of a raise for herself. Her current price for attendance in one of her workshops is $1,500. "I didn't start

instant wisdom
ON BRINGING IN BUSINESS

Sometimes it really is all about whom you know. For many companies, that's how business comes through the door.

Build marketing tasks into your day-to-day business. If you wait until you feel you have time, you might not get around to it.

Sometimes companies who could be considered your competitors are the very people who will send business to you. Don't leave them out of your marketing efforts.

When nothing's happening, do the things you know lead to new business.

If you want to become a successful networker, focus more on what you can give than what you can get. Let it be about other people instead of being all about you.

Plant a lot of seeds and eventually some of them will grow. You may gain a new client years from now from a seed you plant today.

Give yourself a raise. No doubt, you deserve it.

out charging $1,500 for the workshop," she says. "I started at $200 in 1990. In the very beginning, I didn't know if it would work, but I saw that the results for people in the workshop were great, so I immediately went to $350 and then every year I'd give myself a raise." Year by year, her price climbed steadily: $450, $550, $650. "Then I went to $850 and I sort of stuck there for a few years," she says. "Going to the four-figure number was hard. I was like oh, no. That's so much money." But it wasn't an issue of clients balking at paying more—it was an issue Chellie had with herself. "The number one problem that people have in business (especially women): asking for the money and valuing yourself enough." Chellie believes that the lowest price is not the reason people buy or don't buy. "Not unless you're selling a can of peas. But even then, the cheapest might not be the best. I want the top quality, grade A peas. I teach people that in my workshops all the time. The more you value yourself, the more people value you."

Chellie says that, in her experience, people don't question whether she's qualified to charge whatever amount she's currently charging. "No one has ever done that," she says. "You don't go to school to get a degree in financial stress reduction, you know. Let's face it: I made it up." She was asked once in fifteen years whether she had any credentials. She said that her credentials are the results attendees get from her class. She adds, "If you don't get any results, or you don't get the results you came for, then I'll give you a complete refund. But you have to do the work. You can't just sit there like a bump on a log and think it's magic and it's just going to work without you doing anything."

Part of Chellie's ability to be so at ease in the whole process of sales is that she doesn't see it as convincing people so much as helping them. "The way you make money is by serving people," she says. "When you have gifts to give—and everybody has gifts—you can find people who want those gifts and are willing to pay some money for them. And sometimes they're willing to pay a lot of money." ■

🦟 **TAMI SCHNEIDER** is a director of and teacher for Cleveland Yoga (*www. clevelandyoga.com*) in Beachwood, Ohio. Her studio offers athletic yoga classes taught in a heated room.

Before you started your company, what were you clueless about?
Starting a company.

Did it feel like a big risk?
No.

How long was it before you were able to pay yourself?
I was lucky. I've never yet gone without a paycheck. When I don't get one, it's time to shut the doors.

Did you have a business plan?
No.

What do you like best about owning your own company?
Living and dying with my own mistakes.

What do you like least?
My brain never stops thinking.

What would you tell a friend whose company is going through a dry spell?
Try feng shui. Hang a crystal in the southwest corner of your business for financial wellness. Also, place a small box below it with a couple of dollars in it and pray that they mate!

What would you tell someone whose business is growing faster than she can handle?
Give in. Stop trying to do it all. Bite the bullet and pay someone to help.

What's the best advice anybody's ever given you?
Let things unfold naturally.

What's one mistake you won't make twice?
Actually, I've made the same mistake three times: having a partner.

Does your business improve your lifestyle or make it more difficult?
Definitely improves it. I teach yoga and own the studio!

How has owning your own business affected your marriage?
It's strengthened my marriage. I'm not at home waiting for him all the time now.

Could you ever work for someone else again?
Maybe.

What do you think you'll do next?
Retire.

How would a man run your business differently?
He would run it too much like a giant corporation. I like to keep things simple.

❧ **DIANNE MALLERNEE** is the owner of Di's Mountain Get-A-Way (*www. dismountaingetaway.com*) in Blue Ridge, Georgia. Her company rents vacation cabins in the mountains of northwest Georgia.

How did you know it was time to start your own company?
After helping three other companies build their business, a little light went on for me one day. I thought, Why am I doing this for other people? Duh! I need to build my own business.

Did it feel like a big risk?
Yes, and it still does.

How much startup capital did it take?
$50,000.

How do you find clients and customers?
About 85 percent of my customers (renters) come from the Internet. Approximately 75 percent of my clients (cabin owners) come from referrals.

How did you know it was time to hire your first employee?
When I'd been working seventy to eighty hours a week for months. I finally realized it was time to rethink and let someone else help.

How do you know when it's time to fire someone?
When the person seems to think that he is the boss.

What do you tell yourself during slow times?
Basically, when things are slow or not going well, I just turn it all over to God. Then I do my part.

Who are your role models?
Strong women who do their jobs day in and day out—and even on bad days, pick themselves up, brush themselves off, and go on about their business. No pity parties.

What would you tell someone whose business is growing faster than she can handle?
Make sure you put some money aside for a slower time. But enjoy the success of watching it grow.

What would you tell a friend whose company was going through a dry spell?
Step back, look to see what your competitors are doing, and move forward.

What's the best advice anyone ever gave you?
Be yourself. Never try to be anyone else.

What's one mistake you won't make twice?
Taking on a business partner who I thought was a friend. That lasted about an hour and a half.

Does having your own business give you more or less freedom than working for someone else?
It actually works both ways—in the beginning, less freedom, but after a while, more flexibility.

How has owning your business affected your marriage?
I believe it's kept us strong in many ways. We're both self-employed and it's helped us in keeping the lines of communication open. We both fully support each other.

Could you ever go back to working for someone else again?
It would be hard to work for someone else again after being my own boss for so long, and after having the freedom that I'm used to. But if it came down to it, if that was my only choice, then yes. Don't ever think you're too good to go back and work for someone else. ■

If you can imagine it, you can create it.
If you dream it, you can become it.

William Arthur Ward

❧

10

Time to Start Your Own Startup

———

Are you ready to make the jump? It's not easy to voluntarily let go of the security in that steady paycheck. You might feel as if you're about to step off a cliff into thin air. Maybe you don't expect to fall, but you have no visible means of support to catch you either.

Before my first partner and I quit our salaried jobs, we bought a pack of blank index cards and on each card wrote one of the many things we needed to do to start our own agency—from design a logo to find an attorney. The scariest card of the whole deck read "Tell Bob we're quitting." Although the one that came just after that one was pretty frightening in its own right: "Start living without paychecks." Eventually, B.A. and I got up the nerve to make the leap, and we had the time of our lives building MATCH. Neither of us has ever wished that we had hung on to our jobs with Bob.

Losing the company-paid health insurance plan is the number-one lame excuse people give for keeping a bad job instead of bellying up to the bar and starting their own business. Get over it. You are not shackled to The Man for the purposes of being able to take your kid to the doctor from time to time. You can buy an individual or family health insurance policy and still manage to pay your mortgage. Don't be deceived by the astronomical COBRA rates. Shop around online or just call up a good insurance broker and have him or her get you prices on a solid policy with a reputable health insurance company. The cost of your health-care premiums is a small price to pay for your freedom.

Are you an entrepreneurial success story waiting to happen? If you can build a company out of thin air, if you can go out and create business, if you can come up with an idea and make it fly, then what are you waiting for? If it doesn't work, you can always get another job.

I hope you've learned by now that those of us who have managed to pull it off are really nothing extraordinary. Although all of the women interviewed for this book are truly spectacular individuals, they're also just regular people. If you think you can start your own business, you probably can. And if you can gain some wisdom or learn from the mistakes of women who have gone before you, or even just borrow some confidence, then this book will have done its job.

The Startup:
Where Do You Start?

Start with a pad of paper. Make random notes, write lists, capture your ideas, and outline plans. Ask yourself a lot of questions:

- ◆ What do I have to sell?
- ◆ Who needs what I have?

- Who else is trying to sell to them?
- What frustrates those buyers about their current options?
- How would I reach potential buyers?
- What about my company would capture their attention?

Next, jot down some thoughts on money and startup capital:

- How much could I charge?
- What would it cost to create my product or service?
- How would cash flow work?
- How much money would it take to launch my business?
- Where could I get the money?
- How long will it be before I can make a living?
- What changes would enable me to live without a regular salary?
- What hurdles would I have to cross? How can I cross them?

Another thing to consider is your brand. This is how you'll separate yourself from your competitors. Even if you're not planning to spend the millions required to run a TV campaign during the Super Bowl, your communications are still a crucial part of planning your business. Everything you present to the world, from the name of your company to how you answer the phone to what you wear in client meetings, will express the spirit of your brand. How would you describe your company? Compare your company's characteristics to other brands, products, or qualities:

- A Four Seasons or a Hampton Inn?
- An SUV or a convertible?
- Friendly or formal?
- Innovative or traditional?
- Sophisticated or down-to-earth?
- Humorous or elegant?

Start defining the personality of your company before you create the company. A strong brand is how you'll stand out in the marketplace.

Business Plan, Schmizness Plan

Do you need a business plan? That depends on whether you need capital. If you're going to need a large cash infusion from a bank or a venture capital angel or some other source, then yes, they'll want to see a business plan.

But if you're going to self-fund this startup, you may not need to spin your wheels with a business plan. This is not to say that you should quit your job this second and go off half-cocked. But if, for instance, you're starting a simple service business at home, you probably don't need a formal business plan. It certainly won't hurt you to write one, and you definitely should think through the issues addressed in a typical business plan, but a business plan is not necessarily the price of entry. Entry is the price of entry.

If you feel like you're ready to start your business, start it. You don't need anybody's permission.

Let's say you have a general idea of what your company is about and how it would make money. Following are some basic steps you can take before officially launching your new business . . . or, for the procrastinators in the group or those exceedingly quick with a letter of resignation, immediately after you launch it.

Name That Company

Coming up with a name is as good a place to start as any. Naming your company is almost as personal as naming your baby, so follow your own personal gut feelings.

Try to avoid long, generic names, like Affiliated Technology Services. In fact, you might do better to avoid long names altogether because they will invariably get shortened. Affiliated Technology Services will quickly become ATS, or Affiliated, neither of which are very catchy. (You'll definitely want to avoid any multi-word names that would result in embarrassing acronyms, like Provident Integrated Software Service.) Generic industry words in a company name are boring and easy to forget. And you do want your company to be memorable.

If you're planning to form a one-person company, or if you're a freelancer, there's nothing wrong with using your own name: Katherine Blumgarden Design or Jane Doe Consulting. Some people like to attach a catchall word at the end that makes them sound larger, like Sarah Jones & Company or Sarah Jones & Friends.

You might also consider just using an interesting noun. It doesn't have to mean anything. What did Apple Computers mean in the beginning? Yes, people ask where the name came from, but there's nothing wrong with having a built-in conversation starter. (Just make sure you script a good answer, so the conversation doesn't fall flat.)

If you can do it without feeling too silly, audition potential company names by pretending to answer the company phone. ("Hello, this is [insert company name]. Thank you for calling [insert company name].")

Logo á Go-Go

Consider also that your name will take shape in the form of your logo. Designers generally have an easier time working with a short name than a long one, and a descriptive or unusual name might inspire more interesting visual solutions.

One solid piece of advice: Get the best designer you can for your logo. If you can't afford much money, think about offering some sort of trade in services. Or scope out the design students' talents at a local art school. Talent is more important than experience in this case, although it would be a good idea to use a designer who does actually have some logos in his or her portfolio and a familiarity with issues such as the need for it to work in both color and black and white. (What if your gorgeous color letterhead turns out to be unintelligible when faxed?) The designer will probably show you an exploration of several possible logos; probably you'll love one of those and can move on to the next step of building a corporate identity package around your logo.

Your Domain

As soon as you have a company name, reserve an online domain. You'll need it for your company Web site, but even if you don't plan to have a Web site up immediately, you can still use that domain for your e-mail address. Like, *elizabeth@tribecreativeinc.com,* instead of *elizabeth@ somephoneorcablecompany.com.* People tend to assume that e-mail addresses ending in a major utility or ISP are home or family e-mail accounts. That's probably not the impression you want to make when you're e-mailing a hot business lead.

To determine if the domain you want is already taken (and to buy it quickly if it isn't) go to *www.register.com* or any of the other domain registration sites, which you should be able to find easily enough through a search engine. If the .com extension of the name you want is taken, you could investigate the availability of the name using the .net or .biz extension.

www.YourCompanyHere.com

A Web site is one of the most powerful ways to level the playing field between a small startup and larger competitors. And if you don't have one, you may well be the only company on the planet that doesn't. You don't have to have an office for clients to visit, but you really must have a site.

Think of your Web site as an electronic sales brochure. Just the exercise of organizing its components and writing the copy is extremely useful for helping you define your business and what its competitive differences might be.

To get a Web site pulled together, you can go to a company that specializes in developing Web sites (which can be expensive), you can get a free or extremely cheap one from various sources (but you get what you pay for there), or you can find someone who has a small home-based business designing Web sites (quite possibly the best option for a modestly funded startup). A simple site with four or five pages can be done fairly inexpensively and easily. Home-based businesspeople are sometimes willing to work out a trade, if cash is tight. If they don't need what you plan to sell, promise them the bumper crop of summer zucchini from your garden or all the free dog-sitting they can use. If you want to do your own site and you really, seriously have some true design skills (be honest here), *www.godaddy.com* has the best build-your-own-Web-site format of any of the hosting sites (according to word on the street as of this writing).

As with your corporate logo, the caliber of design on your Web site is important. Make sure your Web site is something that makes you proud.

To Inc. or Not to Inc.

The question of whether or not to incorporate is always a biggie for people starting their own companies. Truly, this is one of those questions for which there are at least several right answers. You can spend a lot of time comparing the pros and cons of sole proprietorships, S corps, C corps, and Limited Liability Corporations (LLCs). It's up to you, with the advice of your attorney and CPA, to figure out what's right for your company.

Clients, especially large corporations, often feel more comfortable dealing with corporations. If you think you'll eventually incorporate, do it now so that your business cards, letterhead, Web site, and so on will include that all-important *Inc.*

Let Me Give You My Card

One of the most exciting moments of starting a new company is seeing your logo come to life on freshly printed letterhead and business cards. This is one of those branding areas where even a small home business can set the bar as high as any gigantic and lushly funded company. Your letterhead will be your face to the world, so you want to feel proud of it and excited by it. You don't have to rent Class A office space in a downtown high-rise to play with the big boys and girls, but it does help to have a really cool card.

When you're putting together your initial corporate identity package, think through all the pieces you might need in the course of doing business:

- How often will you write letters?
- Will you write long letters that will require a second sheet? (These are just like your letterhead sheets, but without the address information.)
- Will you be creating PowerPoints or other client meeting materials? (Second sheets are also useful for printing presentations.)
- Will you need some memo paper for more casual handwritten notes that you stick in packages?

- ◆ Do you want pads of sticky notes with your company logo?
- ◆ Which will you use more often—envelopes or mailing labels?

If you're printing a small quantity—say, fewer than 1,000 sheets of letterhead—you might investigate digital printing, which is relatively inexpensive and has advanced in quality over the last several years. Keep in mind, though, that you are sometimes limited to certain types of paper with digital printing. It should be easy to find a good digital printer in your area, or you can work online with a printer such as *www.imagers.com*. If you're printing more than 1,000 in quantity, you'll probably want to use traditional offset printing. Keep in mind that once they turn those presses on, adding another 1,000 sheets now will cost much, much less than printing another 1,000 six months from now. Have your printer give you estimates for several different quantities so you can see how that works. Also, splurge on good paper for your letterhead and cards. It will be worth it.

You may not need all of these pieces for your corporate identity package, but you will want to think through everything you do need so you can save money by printing it all at once. Here are some options to consider:

- ❑ **Business cards.** Consider printing one with the company info but no name, in case you want it for a freelancer representing your company, or to use as an enclosure card for client gifts and flowers. Or, you can print an extra quantity of color shells and then just do a black ink run later to add a new employee's name (a cheap and farsighted add-on.)
- ❑ **Letterhead sheet.** Include your logo, company name, address, and possibly your phone, fax, and Web address.
- ❑ **Second sheet.** This will list your logo and company name but no address or contact info. Second sheets can give a professional, branded look to presentations you crank out at the last minute, print at your desk, and slip into a binder or folder.

❑ **Envelopes.** You will most likely need a standard number-ten business envelope. If your designer made your letterhead sheet an odd shape or size, you'll obviously need an envelope to fit. (Custom-sized envelopes are expensive for printers to construct. Avoid that unless cost is no object.) In most cases, your envelope would include only your logo, company name, and address—no phone numbers or Web address.

❑ **Smaller notepaper or note cards (sometimes called a memo sheet).** If you're planning to use this for handwritten notes to thank clients or business contacts, print on the same quality paper as your business-sized letterhead and include a memo-sized envelope in the print run. If you're thinking of something more like a scratch pad that you would use to scribble a note to toss in an overnight package, then use a thinner, less expensive paper. (Ask your printer about pads of sticky notes with your logo, if you do a lot of those sorts of notes.)

❑ **Mailing labels.** It's a nice thing to have a large color label with your logo, especially if you'll be mailing or couriering business papers.

❑ **Small stickers with your logo.** These are a nice touch for sealing packages and large envelopes. They are fairly inexpensive, as long as you're printing other materials.

When you're running your own business, there will be plenty of frustrations and many perfectly valid reasons for tearing out your hair. Don't add to that list by shortchanging yourself on the proper tools to do your job. Buy the best you can afford of any items you'll need from the following list:

❑ Computers and software

❑ Printer

❑ Business phone with conference and speakerphone capabilities (consider a wireless phone with headset if talking on the phone is a large part of how you'll spend your day)

- ❏ DSL or other high-speed Internet access
- ❏ Fax machine
- ❏ Dedicated phone line for fax machine (don't even think about having your fax share with your regular business line—it's not worth the hassle for clients or customers)
- ❏ Cell phone and/or PDA
- ❏ Voice mail
- ❏ Postal meter
- ❏ Seriously good file cabinets
- ❏ Label maker (who can resist making tidy little labels for all those file folders?)

Finally, be sure to have a complete inventory of office supplies. Don't wait until you need packing tape or fax toner or big mailing envelopes. These are the little things that can drive you crazy if they're not there when you need them. Do yourself a favor and make a big haul from your favorite office supply store, or order online and have it all delivered.

Your World Headquarters

Where will this company of yours live? Many entrepreneurships start out in home offices and then grow into real space down the road. If you decide to work at home, some common and obvious locations are a spare room, a welcoming corner of the basement, or even an uncluttered garage. Think about whether you'll need to host clients or other business contacts for meetings. Many home-based business owners take advantage of a local coffee shop for meetings with just one or two people, or arrange to hold a meeting over lunch at a restaurant. Unless you'll be spending the majority of your time outside the office seeing clients and prospects and vendors, consider that your home office should be exceedingly pleasant—or else you're missing one of the nicest parts of working at home.

The feng shui folks say that if you're in an outgoing people business, you should locate your home office at the front of the house, and if you do introspective work (such as writing) you might be happier in the back of the house.

Consider also the possibility that you might want to put in some early morning or late evening hours when other people in the house are sleeping. (A large percentage of home-office parents do this at least occasionally.) You might not want your office right next door to a light sleeper.

Hey Look, They Already Invented the Wheel

One of the things you'll need to figure out is how work will move through your company. You'll be making up plenty of things as you go along. Take advantage of any process or system you can that someone else has already figured out before you. Preferably before you start work on your first paying assignment, you'll develop a plan for how you'll handle basic financial tasks such as billing your clients and tracking expenses. Many of these processes will be unique to whatever sort of business you're starting, but there are a few universal needs, such as balancing your company checkbook and figuring out whether or not you're making a profit. For this, many small businesses use Intuit's Quickbooks software. There are other software platforms available, but this one is widely accepted, works fairly well, and offers both Mac and PC versions, and you should have an easy time finding a freelance or full-time bookkeeper who can deal with it. Also, the software is enough of a no-brainer that most business owners can set it up by themselves in the beginning, and graduate to outside help as they grow.

If you are starting a service business that traffics professional services or knowledge-based projects (such as advertising, public relations, foreign translations, or almost any other form of brain product), and if you use either a widespread team of freelancers or a tightly knit office of thinkers, you might consider an extranet site such as WorkZone. This site can serve as a virtual office, where you can post work in progress to be accessed by anyone on your team. When everyone is finished with comments and revisions, you move the document to your clients' file for their review. You can find WorkZone at *www.trychys.com.*

How Many Highly Paid Execs Does It Take to Change the Toner?

As an entrepreneur, you might find yourself trying to do a lot of new things that you've never had to do before. Save this gung-ho attitude for figuring out why the printer is jamming. For the big stuff, gather around you the most talented professionals you can afford. Following is a short list of the relationships that will become increasingly important to your success. These will be your critical partners in building your company and trusted advisors in both growth and adversity. You might not need all of them right away, but if you do need them, you'll want to make sure you have the really, really good ones:

- ❑ C.P.A.
- ❑ Bookkeeper
- ❑ Corporate attorney
- ❑ Banker
- ❑ Insurance broker
- ❑ Computer consultant
- ❑ Courier service
- ❑ Overnight delivery service

- ❑ Payroll service
- ❑ Webmaster
- ❑ Ad agency
- ❑ Public relations agency
- ❑ Limousine or car service

The Beauty of Plan B(s)

Even superheroes have backup plans. If Batman is tied up, Robin can swoop in and save the day. When you're a startup, the last thing you want is for your clients or customers to get impatient with you for not being able to make things happen.

Think through your basic systems to figure out what needs to be backed up by an alternative plan. If you use DSL, have a dial-up option in place for times when the DSL service goes out. Buy a cheapie printer to serve as a stand-in when your regular printer gets something stuck in its craw.

If possible, have someone you can call to fill in for you if you get sick or actually decide to take a vacation. This is one of the key benefits of having a business partner or two, but even those flying solo can create a workaround solution for occasional needs.

You'll Sleep Better with a Cash Cushion

Having a financial cushion of cash reserves is a Plan B of tremendous consequence. If you own a business, you are bound to wake up in the middle of the night from time to time, often in a state of cold-sweat panic. Whatever you're worried about, money will solve it nine times out of ten.

If you can remind yourself that you've got those cash reserves, then you will very likely be able to roll over and go back to sleep.

You'll find valuable peace of mind in having three to six months—or even a year—of operating expenses sitting in the bank, drawing some inconsequential amount of interest. Occasionally, despite our best intentions, this is indeed a cruel world. And when it is, a healthy chunk of cash that you can readily access will make you vastly less vulnerable. ∎

🏃 **ANDREA NOVAKOSKI** is president and founder of 2 Places at 1 Time (*www.2placesat1Time.com*), Inc., in Atlanta, Georgia. Her company provides corporate concierge services that are underwritten by employers as an employee benefit.

How did you know it was time to start your own company?
I hated working in corporate America. I knew I could make someone a lot of money and that someone might as well be me. I saw the cost of that option as a lot of hard work and I was never afraid of hard work. So I did it. No regrets.

Did it feel like a big risk?
Not really, because I didn't see failure as an option.

How much startup capital did it take?
$5,000—my life savings at twenty-four.

How long was it until you were able to pay yourself?
Within the first year.

Did you have a formal business plan laid out?
Yes, I went to the library and researched business plans and wrote one for myself. I also hired college students to conduct a market research study that I created prior to starting my company.

Before you started your company, what were you totally clueless about?
How much money it would really take to run my business. I was twenty-four years old. Ignorance is a blessing and a curse.

How do you find clients?
We have been fortunate to receive a lot of positive press. Companies call us from reading our media coverage, find us online, or sometimes [they contact us] because their competitors are our clients.

What's your finest wisdom on how to gain new business?
Be passionate about what you do and creative about how you get the word out.

What's the secret to a successful cash flow?
Be just as serious about collecting as you are about providing an excellent service or product. Front-load contracts and include as much as possible in the contract for the client to fund. We built our initial databases and housed them on our clients' servers and had our clients providing parking, all equipment, and even office supplies.

How did you know it was time to hire your first employee?
When I landed a large corporate client that required full-time staff.

What's the secret to hiring the right people?
Follow your gut. You don't have to justify your decisions to anyone.

How do you motivate or inspire your employees?
We create a lot of lore and tell stories of successes within the company. They see me as human, but with the willingness and drive to push through obstacles for the good and success of the company. I am passionate about the difference we make, and that inspires the staff.

What's the most difficult thing about managing employees?
Recognizing each as different and managing them accordingly.

How do you know when it's time to fire someone?
They negatively impact the corporate culture and climate of your work environment.

What do you read for business inspiration?
I've read numerous business books. A couple of quick reads that stand out are Seth Godin's book *The Idea Virus* and the old favorite, *The E-myth*.

What do you tell yourself during slow times?
Buckle down. Focus on cash flow and sales. Only the strong survive.

What would you tell someone whose business is growing faster than she can handle?
Manage your growth; because if your service or product suffers, your clients will quickly disappear.

What would you tell a friend whose company is going through a dry spell?
Cut costs dramatically and immediately to weather the storm and take a step back to make sure you have made the appropriate changes to address the needs of the current times. People don't just buy it because you sell yourself. You need to be addressing a need.

What's one mistake you won't make twice?
Underfunding my business.

Whom do you talk to when you need advice or a sounding board?
My YEO group (Young Entrepreneur's Organization).

What couldn't you have done without?
The emotional support of a couple of friends.

What do you like best about owning your own company?
The ability to create my own destiny.

What do you like least?
It's the ultimate responsibility—it is hard to leave it at the office.

Describe your best day and your worst day.
The best would be closing a big deal or making a significant difference in a customer's life. The worst was laying off a large number of staff when a large client was bought out.

Does your business improve your lifestyle or make your life more difficult?
It improves my lifestyle.

Does having your own business give you more or less freedom than working for someone else?
More freedom. Less time.

Could you ever work for someone else again?
Honestly, probably not in a traditional sense, only if they gave me a ton of autonomy.

What do you think you'll do next?
Real estate investment and maybe the mommy thing.

Do you have an exit plan?
Yes.

How would a guy run your business differently?
The company would not be as emotionally charged, but he wouldn't have the loyalty and employees going the extra mile. It would be less of a family and more of a job for those employed. Our business is very nebulous. Men like the hard numbers and there really aren't any in our business. We sell with style, anecdotes, and passion. A man would probably make a commodity of our business, which would reduce margins and lower quality. Long story short, a man would surely bastardize it!

LAUREN M. DILLARD is owner and "executive kidologist" of KiddiEvents (*www.kiddievents.com*) in Greensboro, North Carolina. Her company provides timesaving services for parents and children, ranging from party planning to mural painting to tutoring.

How did you know it was time to start your own company?
No other employment satisfied me, so I made it my goal to be happy.

Did it feel like a big risk?
No, it felt like my only option.

How much startup capital did it take?
$350 to $500.

Did you have a formal business plan laid out?
Only in my head, but even there it was formatted and detailed.

Before you started your company, what were you clueless about?
The amount of time one can spend working on the computer.

What's your finest wisdom on developing new business?
Promote, promote, promote. And don't be afraid to give things away.

How do you find customers?
Promote, advertise, and yell it from the rooftops. I'm never afraid to approach people with information about my business.

How did you know it was time to hire your first employee?
My business offers seven services. In order to gain confidence and avoid turning down customers, I had to find employees.

What's your secret to hiring the right people?
Trusting your instincts. And background checks.

How do you inspire or motivate employees?
I ask for their input. That way they know they are part of the team.

What's the toughest thing about managing employees?
Being effective without being insensitive or overbearing.

What's the best advice anybody ever gave you?
Minor setbacks are just that—minor.

Whom do you talk to when you need advice or a sounding board?
My mother and clients I knew well before I had the business.

What do you like best about owning your own business?
Flexibility. And the excitement on people's faces when I tell them about it.

What do you like the least?
That I'll never cross everything off my "to do" list.

Does your business improve your lifestyle or make it more difficult?
It improves my lifestyle. I am happy and always have something to look forward to.

Does having your business give you more or less freedom than working for someone else?
More freedom in respect to what time I have to be up and out, when my meetings are, etc. But also less freedom because I have to constantly

be the owner of KiddiEvents. Going out in sweatpants is no longer an option.

Could you ever work for someone else again?
No.

How would a guy run your business differently?
I can't fathom a guy doing this.

❦ **LAURA BELSEY** is a commercial and film director and the founder of Shadow Pictures (*www.shadowpictures.com*), a New York City–based film and commercial production company.

Did it feel like a big risk to you to start your own business?
No, but I was foolish. I underestimated the responsibilities and how much time, energy, and money it takes.

How much startup capital did it take?
Practically none. I had a reel and a lease on some computers, an editing system, and some other equipment.

Did you have a formal business plan laid out?
Nope. Just jumped in.

How long was it until you were able to pay yourself?
Six months.

Before you started your company, what were you clueless about?
Overhead. I underestimated it. All the little things really add up.

How do you find clients?
I have a strong team of sales reps.

What's the secret to a successful cash flow?
Good credit and clients who pay on time.

How did you know it was time to hire your first employee?
[I hired] right away. I couldn't have done it on my own.

What's the secret to hiring the right people?
Trust your instinct.

How do you motivate or inspire your employees?
Whenever possible, give them challenging and stimulating tasks as well as appreciate the value of their work. Figure out together how they want to grow.

What's the most difficult thing about managing employees?
Friendship. When you start a business, you want to surround yourself with people you know and like. But when there are job performance issues, friendship can make things more difficult. Be sure to separate the personal from the professional, have clear boundaries, and focus on the goal and not the personality.

How do you know when it's time to fire someone?
You cringe when the person enters the room.

Who are your role models?
My ideal role model is the archetypal "good king," like the ruler in the Chinese film *Hero*. He is wise, informed, cautious, fair, honest, and brave. He does the right thing, even when it is a tough decision. You have to know when to fight and when to let go. Lead by example.

What do you read for business inspiration?
The Art of War. Also, the board game Stratego is something I recommend for anybody who is interested in business. It's all about knowing how to use both your strengths and weaknesses. You need a strategy, but you also have to know when and how to adapt.

What do you tell yourself during slow times?
Hang in there. Make a list of things you can do. Take it step by step and just do your best.

What's the best advice anybody ever gave you?

Building a company is essentially creating a brand. Everything you do is a reflection of that brand.

What's one mistake you won't make twice?

I did not always hire the right people and did not take action promptly enough.

What would you tell a friend whose company is going through a dry spell?

Make sure this is what you really want to do. If there is a plan B that seems appealing, consider it. But if this is what you love, your passion, your baby, hang in there. Just try not to get too deep into debt and be realistic about your projections. Be really serious about doing the math.

What would you tell someone whose business is growing faster than they can handle?

You're lucky; enjoy it. Make sure you have a good bookkeeper. And save for a rainy day.

Whom do you talk to when you need advice or a sounding board?

My accountant of fifteen years, who is always looking out for me, like a kind and wise uncle.

What do you like best about owning your company?

The freedom, sense of control, and the creativity. It's an opportunity to apply what I have learned from working with other companies and design a company that suits my needs. I love the idea of building something from the ground up, setting the right foundations, and figuring out how to make it grow. I like the challenge of creating a brand—something that has its own identity, separate from me, that others can identify with and feel a part of.

What do you like least?

The pressure. There is no security net. It can be a financial see-saw and you have to have a stomach for the highs and the lows.

Does your business improve your lifestyle or make your life more difficult?
Both.

How has having your own business affected your marriage?
We work together so there is no line between my business and marriage and it's hard to imagine one without the other.

What do your kids think about what you do?
My daughter is interested, and she likes to see all the new work but gets annoyed when my husband and I talk about business at the table.

Could you ever work for someone else again?
Maybe. I'm a director first, a businessperson second. Directing is something I could never not do.

What do you think you'll do next?
Continue to develop the different aspects of the business. I try to balance expanding the commercial business with my creative long-term endeavors.

How would a guy run your business differently?
As a woman, I have a larger sense of emotional responsibility. The feelings of those around me matter a great deal to me, which is usually a good thing but can backfire. A guy would probably be quicker to fire employees who are not performing well. Patience is an investment; sometimes it can really pay off, sometimes it doesn't. ■

We are shaped and fashioned by what we love.

Johann Wolfgang von Goethe

Epilogue

I come from a long line of entrepreneurs, all of them male. My father started his own architectural firm when he was only a few years out of design school. My paternal grandfather was an engineer who founded a company selling engineering and architectural supplies, along with a new technology called blueprints. My maternal great-grandfather owned the local general store in Edison, Georgia. It was called the Fain Trading Company, and apparently they specialized in blue spotted hogs. My maternal grandfather had a string of Ford dealerships, as well as a local oil company and other small-town concerns.

I call on the wisdom of my elders in all sorts of business situations. I think often of conversations I've had with my father, or of what he'd do about a particular business issue. But I also remember stories he's told me about the things his own father told him. I pass on to my son stories my mother told me about her father, from both his business experience and his political career as a state senator.

There are countless priceless bits of advice floating around in my brain that are one generation removed from me. I never heard my grandfathers say them; I only heard my father or mother repeat them. But it's still advice I can use. Their collective wisdom serves me well.

My hope is that when my son is thinking through tough business problems in his future career, or building a company, or just running a lemonade stand up at the top of our street, he thinks of the way the women in his life, as well as the men, have approached business. That he not only honors his father's innate brilliance and logical approach, but also his mother's imagination and intuition.

That's the best we can hope for, really. That we all learn from each other, from both the men and the women who inspire us, and then do what feels right. And that when our children start their own companies, some years from now, they'll just think of it as running their business as the people they admire. ■

A

advertising, 159–162
    See also marketing
Albert, B. A., 60–61
Alice Goldsmith Ceramics, 19–21
APS, 151–153

B

backup plans, 194
bankruptcy, 144
Baseley, Kirsten, 122–125
Belsey, Laura, 201–204
boss, being the, 107–108
    See also employee management
brand identity, 183–184,
    188–191
business cards, 188–189
business enterprises
    brand identity for, 183–184,
        188–191
    guiding principles for,
        9–18
    naming, 184–185
    reasons women start, 1–5
    risks involved in, 135–137
    startup phase of, 29–38
    steps for launching, 181–195
business partners, 51–59
business plans, 184

C

Campbell, Chellie, 7
    financial setbacks for, 142–146
    time management for, 92–95
    See also Financial Stress Reduction
capital, startup, 183
cash cushions, 194–195
Champion, Delia, 153–154
C. . .is for Chocolate, 103–105
Cleveland Yoga, 176–177
Coffee, Cici, 149–151
community, company as part of,
    9–18
companies. *See* business enterprises
ComputerJobs.com, 155–157
Cook's Warehouse, 125–127
corporate identity, 183–184,
    188–191
Creative Alliance, 74–76
Creative Communications
    Consultants, 98–101

D

D'Avanzo, Claudia Brooks, 98–101
delegation, 119–121
Dillard, Lauren M., 199–201
Di's Mountain Get-A-Way, 177–179
domains, Internet, 186
drive, entrepreneurial, 1–3

E

Ella's Room, 101–103
Embry, Denise Joy, 101–103
employee management, 107–121
    firings, 108, 110–112, 118
    at KooKoo Bear Kids, 115–118
    lack of, at Financial Stress
        Reduction, 118–121
    layoffs and, 110, 138–139, 140
    at PT&Co., 108–115
entrepreneur
    desire to be, 1–3
    reason women become, 3–5
Essig, Sherry, 96–98

F

failure, 135–137
financial crisis
    coping with, 135–137
    faced by Campbell, 142–146
    at KooKoo Bear Kids, 141–142
    at PT&Co., 137–140
financial cushions, 194–195
Financial Stress Reduction, 7
    business partners and, 58–59
    guiding principles of, 15–18
    lack of employees at, 118–121
    marketing efforts of, 169–175
    office environment of, 71–73
    startup phase of, 36–38
    See also Campbell, Chellie
firings, 108, 110–112, 118
Fleur de Lys Floral & Gifts,
    127–131
Flying Biscuit Café, 153–154
Frog, 22–25

G

GAVI International, 122–125
Gay, Kim, 151–153
Gilfillan, Nancy, 155–157
Goldsmith, Alice, 19–21
Grenough, Millie, 25–28
Grenough LLC, 25–28
guiding principles, 9–18

H

Hashorva, Lainey, 147–148
health insurance, 182
Herrick, Barbara, 21–22
home offices, 65–66, 69–73,
    191–192
Houghton, Jody, 131–134

I

incorporation, 187–188

J

Jacobs, Julie, 41–43
Jody Houghton Designs, 131–134
Juneau, Nancy C., 63–64
Juneau Construction Company,
    63–64

K

KiddiEvents, 199–201
Kocina, Robin, 78–81
KooKoo Bear Kids, 6–7
    business partners and, 55–58
    employee management at,
        115–118

financial decisions at, 141–142
guiding principles of, 14–15
marketing efforts of, 166–168
office environment of, 69–71
startup phase of, 33–36
See also Mediate, Tara
Kugelman, Sarah, 43–47

L

layoffs, 110, 138–139, 140
letterheads, 188–189
life, quality of, 85–95
location, 65–73, 191–192
logos, 185–186, 189–190
Loving Touch Animal Center, 39–41

M

Magic Bean Company, 147–148
Mallernee, Dianne, 177–179
management issues
  dealing with employees,
    107–121
  at KooKoo Bear Kids, 115–118
  at PT&Co., 108–115
marketing, 159–162
  brand identity and, 183–184,
    188–191
  by Financial Stress Reduction,
    169–175
  by KooKoo Bear Kids, 166–168
  by PT&Co., 162–166
MATCH, Inc., 30, 52, 60–61, 67,
  108, 136, 160
McFarlane, Marilou, 47–49
McFarlane Marketing, 47–49
Media Solutions, 76–78

Mediate, Tara, 6–7
  time management for, 88–91
  See also KooKoo Bear Kids
Messler, Susan, 61–63
Mid-America Events & Expos, 78–81
Moore, Mary S., 125–127
motherhood, balancing with
  business, 88–91, 116–117
motivation, 1–5

N

names, business, 184–185
Natural Body, 149–151
networking, 171–173
Novakoski, Andrea, 196–199

O

office space, 65–73, 191–192
office supplies, 188–191

P

partnerships, 51–59
planning phase. *See* startup phase
Pounds, Jennifer, 22–25
Priority Ventures Group, 96–98
professional help, 193–194
PT&Co., 6
  business partners and, 52–55
  employee management at, 108–115
  financial setbacks at, 137–140
  guiding principles of, 11–13
  marketing efforts of, 162–166
  office environment of, 67–69
  startup phase of, 30–33
  See also Tanaka, Patrice

Q

quality of life issues, 85–95

R

risk, 135–137
Rosen, Donna, 81–84

S

sales
    at Financial Stress Reduction,
        169–175
    at KooKoo Bear Kids, 166–168
    at PT&Co., 162–166
    ways to boost, 159–162
Scandia Down Shop, 21–22
Schneider, Tami, 176–177
Scoppechio, Debbie, 74–76
setbacks, 135–137
    See also financial crisis
Shadow Pictures, 201–204
Sibley, Patricia C., 76–78
skyn ICELAND, 43–47
Soprano, Celine, 103–105
startup capital, 183
startup phase, 29–30
    business plans and, 184
    business stationary and, 188–191
    cash cushions for, 194–195
    deciding on name, 184–185
    deciding to incorporate, 187–188
    fining brand during, 183–184
    blishing Web presence during,
        6–187
    ancial Stress Reduction,
        '8

for KooKoo Bear Kids, 33–36
location issues and, 191–192
logo design, 185–186
planning needed in, 181–195
for PT&Co., 30–33
work processes during, 192–193
stationary, 188–191

T

Tanaka, Patrice, 6
    time management for, 86–88
    See also PT&Co.
terminations, 108, 110–112, 118
Tilghman, Michelle, 39–41
time management, 85–95
Traffic Management Services, 61–63
2 Places at 1 Time, 196–199

V

vacations, 91, 92–93

W

Waskuch, Sara, 127–131
Web sites, 186–187
work processes, 192–193

Y

York Solutions, 41–43